THE NEW NATURE

THE NEW NATURE

RENALD SHOWERS

FIRST EDITION, JULY 1986

Library of Congress Cataloging-in-Publication Data

Showers, Renald E., 1935–
   The new nature.

   Bibliography: p.
   1. Regeneration (Theology)   2. Christian life—
1960–   I. Title.
BT790.S56   1986   234'.4   85-28443
ISBN 978-1-880976-29-6

PRINTED IN THE UNITED STATES OF AMERICA

This book is dedicated to

LOUIS H. SHOWERS

my brother in the flesh and in the Spirit

and to

MARY JANE

his beloved wife

faithful fellow servants of Christ

CONTENTS

INTRODUCTION

T HE APOSTLE PETER declares that God's divine power has granted to Christians everything that pertains to life and godliness (2 Peter 1:3). This is Peter's way of saying that God has given believers all the equipment necessary to live a godly life. One aspect of that equipment has been called by theologians "the new nature."

This book is a study which deals primarily with the Christian's new nature. It develops a number of concepts concerning this significant subject. Among these are the following: the new nature and the old nature are opposite dispositions toward God; the old nature is a disposition of enmity against God; since enmity against God is sin, the Bible calls the old nature "sin," and some theologians have called it "the sin nature."

The new nature is a favorable disposition toward God. It consists of the law of God written in the human heart. The Holy Spirit places it inside the believer at the moment of regeneration. The new nature is the internal, and therefore superior, way of God administering His eternal moral absolutes with human beings in contrast with the old covenant or Mosaic law, which was the external way of God administering those absolutes.

When man rebelled against God in Eden, he became an "old man" (an unregenerate man). In addition, he willfully took to himself the old nature, and his total being became enslaved by this disposition of enmity against God. In this state of total depravity fallen man received the position of slave to the old nature, and the old nature gained the position of master over him. This condition of slavery obligated unregenerate man to obey the dictates of the old nature.

When a person trusts Jesus Christ to be his Saviour, several major changes happen to him. Firstly, he ceases to be an "old man" (an unregenerate man). Secondly, he loses his position as slave to the old nature, and the old nature loses its position of master over him. This means that he is no longer obligated to obey the sin nature. Thirdly, he becomes a "new man" (a regenerate man). Fourthly, he receives the new nature (a new, favorable disposition toward God consisting of the law of God in his heart). Fifthly, he receives the Holy Spirit as his permanent indweller. All of these changes provide the believer with great potential for living a very different kind of life from that of his unregenerate days.

Although the old nature loses its position of master over the born-again person at the moment of regeneration, it does not leave the believer during his lifetime. It continues to dwell in him until the believer is present with the Lord. The old nature actively tries to exercise controlling power over the Christian, in spite of the fact that it no longer has the right to rule him.

The believer always has the potential for internal, spiritual struggle, because he has two opposing natures dwelling in him: the old nature, which he inherited from Adam through his natural birth, and the new nature, which he received from the Holy Spirit through his supernatural birth (regeneration). The old nature, because it is a disposition of enmity against God, tries to control the believer in opposition to God's rule. The new nature, because it is a favorable disposition toward God (the law of God in the heart), prompts the believer to concur with and will to obey God's rule. It does not, however, give the believer the power necessary to overcome the power of the old nature. The Christian, therefore, needs more than the new nature, if he is to do God's will.

Whenever the believer relies upon the old covenant (Mosaic) law or himself for the power necessary to overcome the power of the old nature, he is defeated. The old nature takes him captive against his will and prevents him from doing the will of God. This does not mean, however, that the believer is doomed to be continuously defeated. At the moment of regeneration the Holy Spirit permanently indwells the believer. He is the source of power necessary to defeat the power of the old nature in the believer.

Because the Holy Spirit permanently indwells, His power is constantly available to the believer. That power will not operate in the Christian's life, however, unless he personally appropriates it by faith. Moment by moment he must trust the Holy Spirit rather than himself to empower him for victory over the power of the old nature.

It is hoped that this study will remove much of the mystery associated with the new nature and give believers a fresh understanding of the radical difference between the unregenerate and the regenerate person.

1

BASIC DEFINITIONS

The Meanings of the Term "Nature"

An Important Consideration

T HE TERMS "old nature" and "new nature" never appear in the Scriptures. They were adopted by theologians to refer to concepts which are presented in God's Word. Having observed the divinely revealed concepts in the Bible, theologians had the task of searching languages to find terms which would accurately represent the biblical concepts. Their choice of terms was determined by the basic meanings of those words.

In light of this process by which the terms old nature and new nature were adopted, an understanding of the biblical concepts represented by them requires an examination of the basic meanings of the words for nature in the original Greek, Latin, and modern English. Accurate definitions of the terms "old nature" and "new nature" cannot be established apart from such an examination.

The Meanings Derived from Languages

The Meanings of the Greek Word for Nature

The Greek word for nature is *phusis*. According to Arndt

and Gingrich, this word, when applied to man, has the following meanings: (1) "natural endowment" or "condition"; (2) "natural characteristics" or "disposition"; and (3) "natural being, product of nature, creature" and "species" and "mankind."[1]

Thayer says that *phusis* means "the sum of innate properties and powers by which one person differs from others, distinctive native peculiarities, natural characteristics."[2]

Moulton and Milligan define *phusis* as " 'innate properties or powers,' what belongs to persons or things in view of their origin." They also found evidence in ancient papyri for *phusis* meaning "kind."[3]

Liddell and Scott claim that *phusis* means a "kind," a "sort," or a "species."[4]

According to Hodge the *phusis*

of anything is the peculiarity of its being, that in virtue of which it is what it is; it is that which belongs to its original constitution, and is opposed to what is taught, acquired, or made. The word is sometimes used for a disposition or sentiment arising out of our nature, as opposed to mere arbitrary rules, as in 1 Corinthians 11:14.[5]

The Zondervan Pictorial Bible Dictionary gives these meanings for *phusis:* (1) "the inherent character of a person or thing (Romans 1:26; 2:14; 11:21-24; I Corinthians 11:14; Galatians 4:8)," (2) "by birth (Romans 2:27; Galatians 2:15; Ephesians 2:3)" and (3) "disposition (2 Peter 1:4)."[6]

The Meanings of the Latin Word for Nature

The Latin word for nature is *natura.* According to *A Latin Dictionary* the basic meanings of this term are as follows: (1) "the natural constitution, property, or quality of a thing" and (2) "of character; nature, natural disposition, inclination, bent, temper, character."[7]

The Meanings of the English Word Nature

The Oxford English Dictionary, the ultimate authority on English words, defines nature in the following ways:

(1) "the essential qualities or properties of a thing; the inherent and inseparable combination of properties essentially pertaining to anything and giving it its fundamental character," (2) "the inherent and innate disposition or character of a person," (3) "the general inherent character or disposition of mankind," (4) "the character or essence of the thing or person" and (5) "the inherent dominating power or impulse (in men or animals) by which action or character is determined, directed, or controlled."[8]

Webster's Third New International Dictionary defines nature in the following ways relevant to this study: " ... 2b: the distinguishing qualities or properties of something (the $\sim$ of mathematics) (the $\sim$ of a literary movement) 3a: the fundamental character, disposition, or temperament of a living being usu. innate and unchangeable ... b: the fundamental character, disposition, or temperament of mankind as a whole: HUMAN NATURE ... c (1): a specified kind of individual character, disposition, or temperament (his kindly $\sim$) ... 4: a creative and controlling agent, force, or principle operating in something and determining wholly or chiefly its constitution, development, and well-being ... b: an inner driving or prompting force (as instinct, appetite, desire) or the sum of such forces in an individual. ... "[9]

The American College Dictionary gives these major meanings for nature when applied to persons or things:

(1) "the particular combination of qualities belonging to a person or thing by birth or constitution; native or inherent character: *the nature of atomic energy,*" (2) "the instincts or inherent tendencies directing conduct: *a man of good nature,*" (3) "character, kind, or sort: *a book of the same nature*" and (4) "a person of a particular character or disposition."[10]

Conclusions Drawn from Languages

On the basis of the meanings quoted above, it appears that languages have assigned two primary definitions to the term nature when applied to persons or things. One could be called *the broad definition,* because it covers an entire combination of properties. The other could be designated *the narrow definition,* because it deals with only one property.

The Broad Definition

The broad definition could be stated as follows: *a nature is that unique combination of attributes which determines the kind of a being or thing in contrast with all other kinds of beings or things.* The heavens and the earth provide habitation for many different kinds of beings and things. There is a distinct difference between God and angels, human beings and plants, elephants and mice, organic and inorganic things, or personal beings and impersonal things. Indeed, there is a great variety of kinds in the universe.

Why is there such a diversity of kinds? What makes one kind different from another kind? The answer is that each kind has a unique nature (a unique combination of attributes) which is peculiar to the members of that kind. Human beings have a nature that is different from the natures of angels, elephants, trees, and all other organic, inorganic, personal, and impersonal beings or things. One could say, then, that nature determines kind.

Since there are many different kinds, and each kind has a unique nature, there are many different natures. Because of this great variety of natures, it has become necessary to assign an adjective to each distinct nature in order to keep its uniqueness in mind. Thus, there are such terms as *human* nature, *divine* nature, and *animal* nature.

It should be noted that "nature" in the broad sense is not synonymous with the term "person." Although every person possesses a nature, a nature and a person are not the same thing. At least two things indicate this. Firstly, every impersonal thing (such as a rock or tree) has a nature but is not a person. Secondly, the incarnated Christ had two complete natures but was only one person.

The Narrow Definition

The narrow definition of nature could be stated as follows: *a nature is that inherent disposition of a being or thing that affects the conduct and character of that being or thing.* In this narrow sense nature is only one property of the broad, total nature of a being or thing. Although it is only one property, it is an extremely crucial one, for it affects every other aspect of the total nature.

That language has attached the narrow meaning of disposition to the term nature is evident from several common expressions. Sometimes the following statements are made concerning a warm, gracious person: "He has a good nature," or "He is good-natured." At other times the same thought is expressed as follows: "He has a good disposition." These expressions make synonyms of the terms nature and disposition. They indicate that language sometimes uses the term nature for a disposition that affects the total being of a person.

The Recognition of Meanings by Theologians

A study of theological writings indicates that theologians have recognized and adopted both the broad and narrow meanings which languages have assigned to the term "nature." For example, Buswell wrote: "In strict definition of our terms, we should hold that *a nature is a complex of attributes.*"[11] In this instance Buswell was referring to the broad definition of nature.

The Lutheran *Formula of Concord* made the following statement:

Since the Fall, man inherits an inborn wicked disposition and inward impurity of heart, evil lusts and propensity; that we all by disposition and nature inherit from Adam such a heart, feeling, and thought as are, according to their highest powers and the light of reason, naturally inclined and disposed directly contrary to God and His chief commandments, yea, that they are enmity against God, especially as regards divine and spiritual things.[12]

Orthodox Lutheran theologians who quote this statement concerning the inborn disposition which is hostile toward God state that the "old nature is hostile to God, seeking its own primary and immediate interest at all cost."[13] They thereby equate the old nature with the evil disposition. This is an example of theologians adopting the narrow definition of nature.

Conclusion Concerning the Old and New Natures

Inasmuch as languages have assigned two primary definitions to the term "nature" when applied to persons and things, it becomes necessary to determine which definition applies to the terms "old nature" and "new nature." Is each of these terms referring to the unique combination of attributes which determines that a human being belongs to mankind, or is each referring to a disposition of man?

It is the conclusion of the author that the old and new natures, as presented in the Scriptures, are dispositions, not total combinations of a human being's attributes. There are several reasons for this conclusion. Firstly, prior to the fall of man Adam did not possess the old nature, but he did possess human nature in the broad sense. He did possess that unique combination of attributes which determined that he was a human being belonging to mankind. When Adam received the old nature through the fall, he continued to be a human being belonging to mankind. He continued to have human nature in the broad sense—the combination of attributes which determined that he was man. Reception of the old nature produced a drastic spiritual change in Adam, but it did not change his inherent kind of being. In other words, it did not produce a metaphysical change. This fact forces the conclusion that the old nature is a disposition rather than a combination of attributes which determines kind. If the old nature were a nature in the broad sense, its reception by Adam would have introduced a new combination of attributes foreign to the original make-up of man. It would have transformed him into something other than a human being.

Secondly, an unregenerate man does not possess the new nature, but he does possess human nature in the broad sense. He does possess that unique combination of attributes which determines that he is a human being belonging to mankind. When an unregenerate man receives the new nature through regeneration, he continues to possess human nature in the broad sense. Reception of the new nature produces a radical spiritual change in him, but it does not change his inherent kind of being. He is called a "new man" (Colossians 3:10), but he is still man. Reception of the new nature does not produce a metaphysical change in a person. This fact forces the conclusion that the new nature is a disposition rather than a combination of attributes which determines kind. If the new nature were a nature in the broad sense, its reception would introduce a new combination of attributes which would transform a person into something other than a human being.

Since a disposition is inherent to the whole nature of man, the reception of a new disposition does not introduce something different to man's metaphysical make-up. It does not involve a metaphysical change.

It should be concluded, then, that the old and new natures are to be defined as dispositions.

2

THE DISPOSITIONS OF MAN
BEFORE AND AFTER THE FALL

The Original Disposition of Man

PRIOR TO THE FALL OF MAN Adam possessed a disposition which was favorably oriented toward God. He fellow-shiped with God and willingly accepted and obeyed His commands. "In the garden before the fall the man and woman acted in accordance with God's command. His will was their law, and they gladly yielded thereto a rejoicing obedience."[1]

Strong states it this way: "Man was created with such a direction of the affections and the will, as constituted God the supreme end of man's being, and constituted man a finite reflection of God's moral attributes."[2] Because man's original disposition was favorably oriented toward God, it has been called a holy disposition.[3]

One thing should be noted concerning Adam's original disposition. It was an unconfirmed disposition. This means that Adam was not locked into his favorable disposition for-ever. He could lose it.

It would appear that the reason that Adam's original disposition was unconfirmed was that Adam himself had never actively chosen this favorable disposition toward God. It had been given to him by God's sovereign choice at man's creation. Since the time of creation Adam had never known anything else, for he had never been confronted with an alternative to being favorably disposed toward God. The first two chapters of Genesis picture God as the active one, taking the initiative to enter into fellowship with and to bestow favor upon Adam. Adam simply received God's advances willingly. In the process he must have become favorably impressed with God, but he never had opportunity to choose actively in favor of Him as opposed to something else.

The Disposition of Fallen Man

Eventually Adam was exposed to a situation in which he was confronted with an alternative to being favorably disposed toward God. In this situation Adam had no other recourse than to make an active choice either in favor of God or against God. It would appear that if he were to choose in favor of God, then he would be confirmed in his favorable disposition toward God forever. Buswell says:

We must postulate that from his condition of probation, by the power of God, through an act of commitment, he might hypothetically have moved into a status of permanent sonship such as is offered to fallen man only through the cross of Christ.[4]

But if Adam were to choose against God, then he would become so thoroughly confirmed in a disposition of enmity against God that nothing short of a divine work of regeneration and reconciliation could rescue him.

The situation came when Satan presented man with a statement that was opposed to God's statement. Satan's statement consisted of two major parts: (1) "You surely shall not die!" (Genesis 3:4), and (2) "in the day you eat from it your eyes will be opened, and you will be like God" (Genesis 3:5). In the first part Satan was assuring Adam that it would not hurt him to disobey God. In the second part he was indicating that active disobedience would benefit man. It would make him become as God. This was Satan's subtle way of saying:

"If you reject the sovereign will of God, you will be your own sovereign."

After hearing the opposing statement, Adam made his choice. It was a choice against God. The opportunity to be his own sovereign was too great to pass by. Therefore, he disobeyed God and fell.

Adam's sin of rebellion consisted of two things: rejection of the sovereignty of God, and an assertion of his own sovereignty. Previously Adam had recognized the sovereign rule of God over his life, but now, in effect, he declared his independence. He desired to be his own sovereign lord. He wanted to run his own life according to his own whims and to do as he pleased. Instead of God being the chief end of man, man was to be the chief end of man. Berkhof says that Adam "placed himself in opposition to God . . . he refused to subject his will to the will of God, to have God determine the course of his life; and . . . he actively attempted to take the matter out of God's hand, and to determine the future for himself."[5]

Adam's nature experienced a drastic change in the fall. It should be noted, however, that the change was not metaphysical in nature. Van Til says:

We know that sin is an attempt on the part of man to cut himself loose from God. But this breaking loose from God could, in the nature of the case, not be metaphysical; if it were, man himself would be destroyed and God's purpose with man would be frustrated. Sin is therefore a breaking loose from God ethically and not metaphysically. Sin is the creature's enmity and rebellion against God but is not an escape from creaturehood.[6]

Sin is exclusively ethical. . . . Sin did not lower man in the scale of being. Sin did not take away from man any of the natural powers that God had given him. Sin did not tend to destroy the metaphysical situation.[7]

In particular sin did not destroy any of the powers that God gave man at the beginning when he endowed him with his image. To be sure here too there have been weakening results. But man still has eyes with which to observe and logical ability with which to order and arrange the things that he observes.[8]

This means that the fall did not change man into something other than man. Adam's human nature in the broad sense remained intact, and he continued to be a full human being as before.

The change that did take place in Adam's nature was as follows: when Adam sinned he lost his favorable disposition toward God and became thoroughly confirmed in a disposition of enmity against God. When man decided to be his own sovereign, he could not tolerate God's claim of sovereignty over him. Thus, he adopted a disposition of enmity against God. One evidence that man adopted such a disposition is the fact that Adam and Eve purposely avoided God when He entered the garden after the fall (Genesis 3:8). Enmity against God is sin. Thus, Van Til says, "Sin is exclusively ethical hostility to God."[9]

Since enmity against God is sin, and fallen man's disposition is characterized by such enmity, it is correct to call that disposition "sin." In conjunction with this Berkhof says that sin "is not to be regarded as a substance infused into the human soul, nor as a change of substance in the metaphysical sense of the word. . . . Sin is an inherent positive disposition toward sin."[10]

In the same vein Eichrodt writes that sin is an "evil habitus."[11] Then he states that a habitus is the same as a disposition.[12] Young declares that in the fall a disposition that was holy changed to one that was unholy.[13]

Since, as noted earlier, man's disposition affects every other aspect of his total nature, Adam's total being was affected adversely by the fall. The sinful disposition caused fallen Adam to begin using every one of his attributes in ways that were contrary to the will of God. Thus, Van Til says that "when we say that sin is ethical we do not mean, however, that sin involved only the will of man and not also his intellect. Sin involved every aspect of man's personality."[14]

When speaking of this tragic condition of Adam, Klooster declares, "He is polluted in every area of his being. Sin takes possession of his heart and makes it exceedingly corrupt (Jeremiah 17:9). Like a cancer sin permeates the whole person, body and soul."[15]

The effect of this influence of the sinful disposition upon every aspect of Adam's total nature was slavery. In Romans 6:16-20 Paul teaches that, as the result of man voluntarily presenting himself to the service of sin in the fall, fallen man was locked into a master slave relationship with his sinful disposition. In that relationship the sinful disposition holds the legal position of master over fallen man, and fallen man holds the position of slave under the sinful disposition. Because of its position of master, the sinful disposition has authority to dominate and control every aspect of fallen man's total nature. Thus, Adam's whole nature became helplessly enslaved in a continuing state of sin.

Theologians use the term "total depravity" for this effect of the sinful disposition upon every aspect of fallen man's total nature. Total depravity does not mean that fallen man will always act as badly as he is capable of acting. Sometimes the sinful disposition will prompt fallen man to live morally and to do kind, humanitarian deeds in order to demonstrate what man can do apart from God. Total depravity does mean that every aspect of fallen man's total nature is controlled by the sinful disposition.

The immediate concomitant of the first sin . . . was the total depravity of human nature. The contagion of his sin at once spread through the entire man, leaving no part of his nature untouched, but vitiating every power and faculty of body.[16]

No better expression of the totally depraved effect of the sinful disposition upon fallen man can be found than that presented in Romans 8:7: "The mind set on the flesh is hostile toward God; for it does not subject itself to the law of God, for it is not even able *to do so.*"

The term "flesh" is used frequently in the Bible to refer to man in contrast with God. God is spirit (John 4:24), but by contrast man is flesh. Robinson says that "flesh represents mere man, man in contrast with God—hence man in his weakness and mortality."[17] It would appear that Paul uses the term in that sense in Romans 8:7. Thus, the mind set on the flesh is the mind set on man. It is the man-centered mind rather than the God-centered mind. It is the mind that sees man rather than God as the chief end of man.

Earlier it was noted that the disposition which man adopted in the fall was a disposition of enmity against God. Inasmuch as the mind set on the flesh is also hostile toward God, it would appear that Paul either uses that expression to refer to the sinful disposition of fallen man or implies that the sinful disposition prompts the mind set on the flesh. Concerning the mind set on the flesh, Murray writes:

Enmity toward God is the actuating principle and governing propension of the mind of the flesh. And when we keep in view what is meant by "mind" in this connection the implication is that the disposition underlying all activity is one of opposition to and hatred of God.[18]

Paul presents the twofold effect of the disposition of enmity. The mind set on the flesh (1) refuses to subject itself to divine law, and (2) it finds itself incapable of such subjection. Concerning the first effect, since the law of God is an expression of God's sovereign rule over man and since fallen man is disposed to reject God's sovereign rule, fallen man refuses to submit to divine law. Haldane indicates that the disposition of fallen man "has a rooted aversion to the spiritual law of God, and admits not its claim to perfect and unceasing obedience."[19]

Concerning the second effect, Haldane writes:

Not only is it a matter of fact that the carnal mind is not subject to the law of God, but such subjection is impossible. Sin cannot be in subjection to the law. This would be a contradiction in terms. For, so far as it would be subject to the law, it would be holy. If, then, sin is essentially, and in direct terms, contrary to holiness, the sinful nature can never yield subjection to the holy law.[20]

Murray expresses it this way:

The last clause, "neither indeed can it be," points to the impossibility that resides in the mind of the flesh and means nothing less than that it is a moral and psychological impossibility for those who are "in the flesh" to have any disposition of obedience . . . to the will of God.[21]

Murray summarizes the teaching of Romans 8:7 as follows:

In the whole passage we have the biblical basis for the doctrines of total depravity and total inability. . . . "Enmity against God" is nothing other than total depravity and "cannot please God" nothing less than total inability.[22]

Because the first man experienced this drastic, confirmed change of disposition, and because man reproduces after his kind, each of Adam's descendants by natural propagation has been born with a sinful disposition. For this reason David wrote: "Behold, I was brought forth in iniquity, and in sin my mother conceived me" (Psalm 51:5).

Berkhof declares that:

As a result of the fall the father of the race could only pass on a depraved human nature to his offspring. From that unholy source sin flows on as an impure stream to all the generations of men, polluting everyone and everything with which it comes in contact.[23]

This means that with the exception of Christ every human

being born since Adam was *born* a sinner. No one has *become* a sinner after birth through some wrong attitude or action of his own. For this reason the Apostle Paul wrote that the unregenerate are "by nature children of wrath" (Ephesians 2:3).

It is because he already is a sinner by nature that each person thinks wrong thoughts and performs wrong actions (Matthew 12:33-35; 23:25-28). Thus, Eichrodt says, "Individual actions, as affronts to the divine will, point to a perverted direction of the human will. *Behind sin stands sin, in the sense of a wrong condition of human nature.*"[24] Again he writes, "Sin is not a matter of occasional deviation from the right way, but of *the consistent outcome of the natural tendency of his being,* which is already planted in him by the inheritance passed on to him at his birth."[25]

Conclusions

In the previous chapter it was seen that the term "nature" in the narrow sense is equivalent to a person's disposition. In the present chapter it has been demonstrated that fallen man's disposition could be called "sin." Taken together these two factors indicate that it would be proper to call unregenerate man's disposition "the sin nature."

This chapter also indicated that fallen man's disposition has placed him in a serious predicament. It has enslaved him so thoroughly in a state of depravity that he is totally incapable of changing his condition. What unregenerate man needs is someone else to redeem him from this slavery and to give him a confirmed new disposition or new nature which is favorably oriented toward God. The rest of this study will show that God in grace has provided such redemption and a new nature for man.

Because the nature that God gives to a person sometime *after* he is born (at the time of regeneration) is called "new," it is proper to call the sin nature with which he is born "the old nature." Thus, the sinful disposition, the sin nature, and the old nature are all the same thing.

3

THE NEW DISPOSITION AND OLD TESTAMENT PROPHECY

An Examination of Key Passages

THE NEW DISPOSITION OR NATURE which is favorably oriented toward God is described in several key prophetic passages in the Old Testament. In order to understand more fully the nature of the new disposition, it is necessary to examine these passages.

Jeremiah 31:31-34

The most outstanding prophetic passage which relates to the new disposition is Jeremiah 31:31-34. The examination of the key passages will begin with it.

The Promise of the New Covenant

"Behold, days are coming," declares the LORD, "when I will make a new covenant with the house of Israel and with the house of Judah" (Jeremiah 31:31).

Several things should be noted concerning this promise of the new covenant. Firstly, the fact that God calls the future covenant "new" implies four things: (1) another covenant was already in existence, (2) by contrast that other covenant could be called the "old covenant," (3) eventually the old covenant would be replaced by the new one, and (4) the old covenant was inadequate in some way. The third and fourth implications are recognized by the writer to the Hebrews:

For if that first *covenant* had been faultless, there would have been no occasion sought for a second. . . . When He said, "A new *covenant*," He has made the first obsolete. But whatever is becoming obsolete and growing old is ready to disappear (Hebrews 8:7,13).

Secondly, it should be noted that the new covenant was to be made with Israel and Judah. The context makes this evident as pointed out by Henderson:

That the Jews as a people, literally taken, are intended . . . must be conclusively evident to everyone who impartially examines the context. The subject of this and the preceding chapter is the restoration of the Hebrews, who are repeatedly, as elsewhere, designated *the house of Judah* and *the house of Israel,* chap. xxx. 3,4; xxxi. 27,31; *Jacob* and *Israel,* xxx. 7,10,18; xxxi. 1,4,7,10,11,23,24,36. It would be doing violence to one of the first principles of hermeneutical consistency to explain these terms, restricted as they are in the passages referred to, by various adjuncts applicable only to the Hebrews, of the subjects of the Messiah's kingdom indiscriminately. Nor can anything be more glaringly incongruous than to give to the language *the house of Judah and the house Israel,* ver. 31, a different interpretation from that which is given to the same language as occuring in ver. 27, where it is universally admitted the literal Israel are [*sic*] meant.[1]

The Description of the Old Covenant

"Not like the covenant which I made with their fathers in the day I took them by the hand to bring them out of the land of Egypt, My covenant which they broke, although I was a husband to them," declares the LORD (Jeremiah 31:32).

God identifies the old covenant as the one which He made with Israel during the time of the exodus. Because the old covenant was given through Moses, it is proper to call it the Mosaic covenant and its law the Mosaic law. The law of the covenant contained the Ten Commandments, the moral aspect of the Mosaic law which had been inscribed on tables of stone (Exodus 20:1-17; 24:12; 31:18; 32:15-16; 34:1,28).

God indicates that Israel broke the old covenant in spite of the fact that He played the role of a husband to the nation (cf. Ezekiel 16). He makes it clear that the whole responsibility for failure rested with the Israelites.

Why did Israel break the old covenant so consistently in spite of God's faithfulness to the nation? Before this question can be answered satisfactorily one fact must be noted: the majority of Israelites who were in covenant relationship with God through the old covenant were unregenerate people. When God initiated the covenant, He established it with every Israelite in the nation at that time, including the regenerate and unregenerate. Laetsch declares that the covenant included "all Israelites, believers and unbelievers, that had been delivered out of Egypt."[2] In addition, each new generation of Israelites automatically came into this old covenant relationship with God by virtue of their physical birth and external circumcision.[3]

Because the majority of Israelites were unregenerate, they were enslaved by their confirmed, sinful dispositions of enmity against God. As a result, not only did they refuse to keep the divine law of the covenant, but also they found themselves totally helpless to keep it (Romans 8:7). Jeremiah had a graphic way of describing their inherent disposition to sin: "The sin of Judah is written down with an iron stylus; with a diamond point it is engraved upon the tablet of their heart" (Jeremiah 17:1). The idea is that sin has been inscribed so indelibly upon their hearts that it is their governing disposition.[4]

Concerning this statement of Jeremiah, Laetsch says that

God, "The searcher of the heart (Jeremiah 17:10) reads there the declaration of their independence from the rule of the Lord."[5]

Another aspect of the reason why Israel broke the old covenant is this: that covenant did not change the corrupt inward nature of the Israelites. The nature of the old covenant law can be described with one word: *external.* While sin was inscribed internally on the hearts of the unregenerate, the law was inscribed externally on tables of stone. As a result, the law was not part of the internal nature which affects the will, thoughts, and actions. It was constantly opposed inwardly by the sinful disposition. The Israelites were *under* the law, but the law was not *in* the unregenerate.

The external nature of the old covenant has been stressed by different writers. Jamieson, Fausset, and Brown state that "in the old dispensation the law was written only on tables of stone; it was but an external rule, affording no power for its fulfillment."[6]

Cowles says that "those agencies were mainly external; the law itself was written on tables of stone."[7]

Although the old covenant law was external in nature, it would be wrong to conclude that it was concerned only about the outward man and not the internal disposition. It recognized that without a right disposition in the heart the Israelites would not love God and keep His commandments (Deuteronomy 5:29). Therefore, its spokesmen commanded the people to love and obey the Lord with all their heart and soul (Deuteronomy 30:1-6) and to make themselves a new heart and a new spirit (Ezekiel 18:31). They reminded them that God looks on the heart (1 Samuel 16:7); it is with the heart that the law must be kept (Proverbs 3:1); it is the heart that determines the issues of life (Proverbs 4:23); delight in God's will can come only by having the law in the heart (Psalm 40:8); Israel's problem was that of a rebellious heart (Jeremiah 5:23). Therefore, the Israelites needed to experience circumcision of the heart (Jeremiah 4:4).

But what was meant by circumcision of the heart? Gaebelein declares that "the circumcision of the heart means regeneration."[8] That this is so is substantiated by Paul in Romans 2:28-29 where he declares that circumcision of the heart is done by the Spirit. Certainly the work of the Spirit which changes the human heart is regeneration.

Because of their enslavement by their sinful dispositions the unregenerate Israelites needed regeneration, but the old covenant did not provide regeneration. Although the old covenant law emphasized the need for an internal change, it did not produce that change. It stood outside the Israelites and demanded conformity to the will of God, but it provided neither the will nor the power needed internally to conform. This is not to say that regeneration was unavailable to people who lived under the old covenant economy, but it is to say that regeneration did not come *because of* the old covenant relationship. That covenant relationship with God did not guarantee regeneration. Calvin expressed it this way: "The Law then is dead and destitute of the Spirit of regeneration."[9]

On final thing should be noted concerning the description of the old covenant: it was considerably different from what the new covenant would be. With regard to this difference, Habel writes:

The "new," which God alone could introduce, would break sharply with the past. This "new covenant" stood in contrast to all past renewals (for example, 2 Kings 23:1-3) of the covenant. This new covenant can hardly be defined in terms of the old. . . . The "not like" of v. 32 makes this antithesis explicit.[10]

The Description of the New Covenant

"But this is the covenant which I will make with the house of Israel after those days," declares the LORD, "I will put My law within them, and on their heart I will write it; and I will be their God, and they shall be My people. "And they shall not teach again, each man his neighbor and each man his brother, saying, 'Know the LORD,' for they shall all know Me, from the least of them," declares the LORD (Jeremiah 31:33-34).

Several things should be noted concerning this descrip-tion of the new covenant. The new covenant will affect the hearts of the Israelites in a way that the old covenant never did. In order to appreciate what is being promised, it is necessary to examine what is meant by "the heart." A study of the Scriptures indicates that the heart, when considered figuratively, is the inner control center of the human being. Out of it flow all the issues of life (Proverbs 4:23). It is the location of human character (Luke 6:45); therefore, it is the aspect of man about which God is most concerned (1 Samuel 16:7; 1 Thessalonians 2:4). The heart serves as the seat of all the spiritual (Proverbs 3:5), moral (Mark 7:20-23), intellectual (Hebrews 4:12), volitional (Daniel 1:8), and emotional (Prov-erbs 15:13) aspects of man's life. Thus such things as the human will (2 Corinthians 9:7) and lust (Romans 1:24) func-tion through the heart.

In Romans 7:8 Paul teaches that lust is produced by the sinful disposition. Inasmuch as the sinful disposition produces lust, and since lust functions through the heart, it can be concluded that the heart is the seat of man's disposition and that the disposition functions through the heart.

It is because the heart is the seat of man's disposition that Bridges declares that the heart "is the great vital spring of the soul, the fountain of actions, the centre and seat of principle, both of sin and of holiness (Matthew 12:34-35)."[11] In light of this it is not surprising to find that the Hebrew word for heart is "especially linked therefore with . . . *the element of responsibility.*"[12] For this reason Behm writes: "Thus the heart is supremely the one centre in man to which God turns, in which the religious life is rooted, which determines moral conduct."[13]

What does God promise to do to the hearts (the inner

control centers) of the Israelites under the new covenant? Since the heart is the seat of the disposition and therefore the place where moral conduct is determined, God promises to write His law in their hearts. Inasmuch as the old covenant law failed to produce obedience because it was *external* and was opposed by an *internal,* sinful disposition, God expresses His determination to correct that situation. Under the new covenant He will *internalize* His law, making it part of the inward nature of His people. Because this promise is the most crucial part of the new covenant, the statements of several writers concerning it are important.

Bruce declares that:

Jeremiah's words imply the receiving of a new heart by the people.[14]

When first they heard the covenant-law they said: "All that Jehovah hath spoken will we do, and be obedient" (Exodus 24:7). But they did not have the moral power to match their good intention. Hence the necessity arose of repeatedly returning to their God and His covenant, only to turn aside to their own ways once again. The defect did not lie in the covenant-law; it was good in itself but, to borrow Paul's language, "it was weak through the flesh" (Romans 8:3)—because of the inadequacy of the human material which it had to work upon. What was needed was a new nature, a heart liberated from its bondage to sin, a heart which not only spontaneously knew and loved the will of God but had the power to do it.

The new covenant was a new one because it could impart this new heart.[15]

Bennett writes:

The inner law, written on the heart, is in contrast to Mosaic ordinances. It has, therefore, two essential characteristics: first, it governs life, not by fixed external regulations, but by the continual control of heart and conscience by the Divine Spirit; secondly, obedience is rendered to the Divine Will, not from external compulsion, but because man's inmost nature is possessed by entire loyalty to God. The new law involves no alteration of the standards of morality or of theological doctrine, but it lays stress on the spiritual character of man's relation to God.[16]

Jehovah no longer seeks to ensure their fidelity by an external law, with its alternate threats and promises: He will rather control the inner life by His grace.[17]

Habel comments:

"The new covenant, however, will not have an external set of laws, no decalog inscribed in stone, but an innate sensitivity to the will of God. The law will be part of man's nature."[18]

Hengstenberg regards this writing of the law in the heart as equivalent to participation in the holy nature of God:

The Law is the expression of God's nature; it is only by the Law being written in the heart that man can become a partaker of God's nature; that His name can be sanctified in him. And it is this participation in the nature of God, this sanctification of God's name, which forms the foundation of: "I will be their God, and they shall be my people."[19]

From what has been seen thus far it would be proper to conclude that the law of God in the heart is equivalent to a new disposition that God puts in the heart of man as an expression of His own holy nature. That the internalized law of Jeremiah 31:33 is a new disposition has been recognized by several writers. Henry says that God "works in them a disposition to obedience, a conformity of thought and affection to the rules of the divine law, as that of the copy to the original."[20] Gray declares that God is "giving them right principles, and a right disposition, so that obedience shall become easy to them."[21]

Since, as was seen earlier, the term "nature" in its narrow sense refers to disposition, this new disposition which God promises in the new covenant could be called "the new nature." Adeney states that the internalized law "would be rooted in the affections of men, and grow up within them as a second nature."[22]

The second thing to be noted concerning the description of the new covenant is this: one of the major results of God internalizing the law will be universal knowledge of Jehovah throughout the nation of Israel (Jeremiah 31:34). What kind of knowledge does God have in mind here? Bruce answers this question:

The knowledge of God as a matter of personal experience is evidently regarded in Jeremiah's oracle as something beyond what the old covenant provided. There was a sense in which the people of Israel knew their God, because He had revealed Himself to them, by contrast with the nations that did not know Him; but even Israel tended to forget Him. . . . But now it is not simply a national acknowledgement of God and His covenant that is envisaged. . . . It is a personal knowledge of God such as marked Jeremiah himself, a personal knowledge of God to be possessed by each individual member of the covenant community, because of the new heart received by each.[23]

Keil writes:

The knowledge of Jahweh, of which the prophet speaks, is not the theoretic knowledge which is imparted and acquired by means of religious instruction; it is rather knowledge of divine grace based upon the inward experience of the heart, which knowledge the Holy Spirit works in the heart.[24]

This kind of knowledge comes only through a salvation experience. Because this is so, Laetsch declares that "to know the Lord is saving faith (Jeremiah 9:24; John 17:3; Galatians 4:8-9), the basic and indispensable essential of membership in God's new covenant."[25]

Since salvation cannot take place apart from regeneration, it would appear that God's writing of the law in the heart involves the regenerating work of the Holy Spirit. Adeney recognizes this to be so, for he calls the writing of the law in the heart "the new birth."[26]

Calvin acknowledges the same, for he declares that Jeremiah 31:33 deals with "the grace of regeneration."[27]

The third thing to be noted concerning the description of the new covenant is this: since the new covenant involves the regeneration of the human heart, only regenerate people can be involved in the new covenant relationship with God. This is radically different from the old covenant which involved many unregenerate Israelites in covenant relationship with God. Physical birth and circumcision brought an Israelite into the old covenant relationship, but a new, spiritual birth is necessary to bring one into the new covenant relationship. Laetsch comments: "The old covenant embraced all the physical descendants of Israel, the new covenant all those that know the Lord . . . only believers."[28]

In light of the second and third things noted concerning the description of the new covenant, it can be concluded that the new disposition is imparted to human beings through the regenerating work of the Holy Spirit.

The Basis of the New Covenant

"For I will forgive their iniquity, and their sin I will remember no more" (Jeremiah 31:34).

God reveals what will make the new covenant relationship possible: His amazing grace that will forgive the sins of the people of Israel and will blot those sins out of His memory. Concerning this basis of the new covenant, Laetsch writes:

There is no work of man, no self-acquired holiness as a condition for entering this covenant. The new covenant has a sacrifice which alone can procure what the ever-repeated sacrifices of the old covenant typified and foreshadowed, the perfect sacrifice of the woman's seed, the Suffering Servant, the Righteous Branch, the Lord Our Righteousness. The Hebrew imperfects "I will forgive, not remember" denote the ever-repeated forgiveness, "richly and daily," and the daily blotting out from God's memory of the sins.[29]

Thus, there is another point of contrast between the two covenants. Under the old covenant the sins of the people were remembered repeatedly; thus the necessity of repeated sacrifices. Under the new covenant the sins will be forgiven and forgotten by God—not just the sins committed before entering the new covenant relationship, but also the sins committed after entering it. It is this ever-repeated forgiving and forgetting by God that will make the relationship possible and will make it last forever. The old covenant relationship would come to an end; the new covenant relationship will never end. This is pure grace—all made possible by God through the perfect, once-for-all sacrifice of the promised Redeemer.

Since the new covenant relationship will never end, and since the new disposition is a crucial aspect of that relationship, it is evident that the new disposition is a confirmed disposition. The regenerate man will have it forever.

Conclusion

On the basis of all that has been seen in this great prophecy of Jeremiah, the following conclusion can be drawn: *the new nature is the confirmed new disposition, consisting of the law of God in the heart, which God places inside a human being through the regenerating work of the Holy Spirit.*

Ezekiel 36:25-28 and 11:19-20

Ezekiel gives two key passages which concern the new nature or disposition. Since the Ezekiel 36 passage contains the same basic material as the Ezekiel 11 passage plus more, attention will be focused upon the former.

The Promise of Cleansing

"Then I will sprinkle clean water on you, and you will be clean; I will cleanse you from all your filthiness and from all your idols" (Ezekiel 36:25). Here God promises to cleanse Israel. Eichrodt insists that the term water is used purely as a symbol of God's cleansing action. It is not referring to a ritual in which water is actually used.[30]

Feinberg claims that the cleansing promised refers to justification, not sanctification.[31] This is correct, for the context indicates that this cleansing will take place when Israel repents and God restores it with great blessing to its land in conjunction with the establishment of the millennial kingdom. In Romans 11:25-27 Paul indicates that Israel will experience salvation or removal of sins, not sanctification, at that time. Zechariah 12:9—13:1 teaches the same.

It would appear that this promise of cleansing corresponds with the promise of forgiveness and forgetting of sins examined in Jeremiah 31:34.

The Promise of a New Heart and New Spirit

"Moreover, I will give you a new heart and put a new spirit within you; and I will remove the heart of stone from your flesh and give you a heart of flesh" (Ezekiel 36:26).

The next things which God promises to the Israelites are: to remove their old heart, to replace it with a new heart, and to put a new spirit within them. He describes the old heart (the unregenerate inner control center) as the heart of stone. Just as stone will not and cannot conform to the shape of another object which is pressed against it, so the unregenerate heart will not and cannot conform to the rule of God (Romans 8:7). As noted earlier, the cause of this hardened condition is the sinful disposition which enslaves the unregenerate heart (Jeremiah 17:1).

The sinful disposition is not the unregenerate heart.

Instead, it is the master of that heart. Thus God's promise to remove the heart of stone is not a commitment to remove the sinful disposition at the moment of regeneration. Rather, it is a commitment to remove the hardened condition of a person's inner control center when the new birth takes place. Obviously, since the sinful disposition's enslavement of the unregenerate heart is the cause of this hardened condition, the removal of the stony condition requires a radical change of relationship between the person and his sinful disposition at the moment of regeneration. The exact nature of this change of relationship will be seen later when the teaching of Romans 6 is examined.

God describes the new heart (the regenerate inner control center) as a heart of flesh. Just as flesh will conform to the shape of another object which is pressed against it, so the regenerate heart is conformable to the rule of God.

The Israelites will receive a new heart because God also promises to put a new spirit within them. At first glance one might think that this is a reference to the Holy Spirit. However, in the next verse God promises to place His Spirit within them in addition to this new spirit. It is evident, then, that the new spirit is a new human spirit, not the Holy Spirit. Eichrodt declares that "the spirit of the individual man . . . is to be distinguished sharply from the concept of the Spirit of God."[32]

The heart (inner control center) serves as the seat and center of the human spirit,[33] and the spirit functions through the heart.[34] Several quotations will indicate what is meant by the term "spirit" in this verse. Ellison declares that the term "tends to mean his dominant disposition, even an overmastering inclination."[35]

Snaith claims that "spirit" is used "to denote the dominant impulse or disposition of an individual."[36] It is "that in a man which dominates him so as to ensure particular type of action . . . being part of the man himself, the controlling element in him."[37]

Eichrodt contends that in Ezekiel "spirit" means: "an

organ of spiritual life in general, synonymous with 'sense' or 'disposition,' the activity of which is to a very large extent concerned with the ethical determination of the human spirit."[38]

From these quotations it is evident that when God talks about a new spirit He is referring to a new disposition. Since, as noted earlier, the new disposition is the new nature, the new spirit promised here is also the new nature. For this reason, Maclaren says that this promise of God refers to "the impartation of a new nature."[39]

This means that the promise contained in this verse corresponds with the promise of the law of God in the heart found in Jeremiah 31:33.[40] It also means that God is referring to what will come through regeneration. Evidence for this is presented by Feinberg who writes:

When the Lord Jesus Christ was interviewed by Nicodemus (John 3), He stated that His inquirer should have known the truth of the new birth. But where is this truth stated? It is here. . . . The new heart, the heart of flesh, and the new spirit can be realized only through the new birth, a birth from above. Thus are new creatures created unto God (2 Corinthians 5:17).[41]

The Promise of the Holy Spirit

"And I will put My Spirit within you" (Ezekiel 36:27). Not only will God give the Israelites a new human spirit, but also He promises to put the Holy Spirit inside them. Maclaren says: "The promise does not merely offer the influence of a divine spirit, working on men as from without, or coming down upon them as an afflatus, but the actual planting of God's Spirit in the deep places of theirs."[42] This is something that Jeremiah did not mention.

As a result of the Holy Spirit indwelling the Israelites, they will have at their disposal divine power to carry out God's will. Davidson states that "there always attaches to 'spirit' the idea of power in operation, the spirit of God exerting power."[43]

Snaith declares:

The idea of a more-than-human power runs through the whole of the use of the phrase [Spirit of the Lord]. As a result of this special endowment of divine power men are able to do that which, in the ordinary way and relying upon purely human resources, they are quite unable to do.[44]

The implication of all this is that the Holy Spirit will work together with the new human spirit for the performance of God's will. The new spirit or disposition will give the regenerate man "the desire and urge to do God's will."[45] The Holy Spirit will give him the power to do God's will.

Mork declares that the Israelites will obey God "by means of their renewed" spirit "as well as God's" Spirit. "There is no idea here of a substitution of God's" Spirit "for man's, but of a cooperation. Before God gives His" Spirit, "He must first give man a renewed, receptive" spirit.[46]

The Result of the Promises

"And I will . . . cause you to walk in My statutes, and you will be careful to observe My ordinances" (Ezekiel 36:27). As a result of God forgiving the Israelites and giving them a new human spirit and the Holy Spirit, they will obey His will. Feinberg says that "as soon as the new life is imparted the new nature manifests itself in a new walk and fruit for God. The statutes and ordinances of God, formerly rejected and broken, will now be fulfilled in the new life."[47]

Plumptre comments:

There follows a spirit of filial loyalty. Possessing this new nature, God's law will become a delight. The sentiment of David is reproduced in them: "Oh, how I love Thy law!" Better still; they learn to say, like Jesus, "I delight to do Thy will, O God!" The path of obedience now becomes a fascination—a flowery mead or a fragrant grove.[48]

It is important to note what is meant by "statutes" and "ordinances." Davidson says that they "are not the mere external enactments of the law; they embrace all the moral laws to which Ezek. so often refers (e.g., ch. xviii., xxii., xxxiii.), and it is doubtful if the prophet refers specially to written laws at all."[49] In other words, these terms refer, not to some specific expression of God's moral rule, but to His moral rule in general. As a result of receiving the new disposition and the Holy Spirit, the Israelites will submit obediently to God's rule.

Although it is the people who do the walking and observing, it is God who prompts and enables them to do it. "The phrase 'cause you to walk' (ver. 27) is very strong in the Hebrew, almost 'I will bring it about that ye walk.' "[50] God does this by providing the equipment necessary to live a godly life—namely, the new disposition and the Holy Spirit.

Because Israel will render obedience, God declares: "So you will be My people, and I will be your God" (Ezekiel 36:28). This corresponds with one of the promised results of the new covenant in Jeremiah 31:33.

Conclusions from the Key Passages

From these key passages it has been learned that God, as the result of the perfect sacrifice of the Redeemer, will forgive and forget Israel's sins and enter into a permanent new covenant relationship with it. This new covenant relationship will be superior to the old covenant relationship, for it will put a new disposition or spirit and the Holy Spirit inside the Israelites, thereby producing their obedience to the will of God. This new disposition will consist of the law of God written in the heart. It is what theologians have come to call "the new nature."

It can be said, then, that "both Jeremiah and Ezekiel think not in terms of a fresh offer of the old Sinai covenant, as does Deuteronomy, but in terms of a *new* covenant, and of a transformation of human nature."[51]

4

THE NEW DISPOSITION, THE WORK OF THE LAW IN GENTILE HEARTS, AND REGENERATION

The New Disposition and the Work of the Law in Gentile Hearts

IN ROMANS 2 the Apostle Paul makes an interesting statement:

> For when Gentiles who do not have the Law do instinctively the things of the Law, these, not having the Law, are a law to themselves, in that they show the work of the Law written in their hearts, their conscience bearing witness, and their thoughts alternately accusing or else defending them (Romans 2:14-15).

The words of the expression "the work of the law written in their hearts" are quite similar to the words that God used in His description of the new covenant in Jeremiah 31:33. This similarity of words prompts a question: Is the work of the law in Gentile hearts to which Paul referred the same as the law of God in the heart of the new covenant?

For several reasons it must be concluded that it is *not* the same. Firstly, it should be noted that "Paul is most exact. He does not say that 'law' is written in their hearts . . . but 'the work of the law.' "[1] Just as there is a difference between a man and the work of that man, so there is a difference between the law and the work of the law.

Secondly, Paul is referring to something that unregenerate Gentiles possess,[2] but, as seen earlier, the law in the heart of the new covenant comes only through regeneration. "God in regenerating grace certainly gives something more than that which the heathen already have."[3]

Thirdly, since, as Paul declares, the unregenerate Gentiles sometimes do the things of the law instinctively or by nature, the work of the law in their hearts must be something common to all of humanity. Thus, the unregenerate Jews must also possess it by nature. If the unregenerate Jews already possess it by nature, and if it is the same as the law in the heart of the new covenant, then there is no need for the new covenant.

In Romans 2:14-15 Paul is teaching that unregenerate Gentiles have a moral consciousness, a sense of right and wrong, inherent within them. They do not have this as a result of an external law, such as the old covenant law, being revealed to them. Nor have they learned it through a process of education. Instead, they possess it as an inherent attribute of their total human nature.

That unregenerate Gentiles do possess an inherent moral consciousness is attested by three things: (1) historically they have made laws condemning such things as murder and theft; (2) they possess a conscience; (3) they sometimes find it necessary to condemn or to justify their actions in their own minds.

It can be concluded, then, that unregenerate Gentiles do have an inherent moral consciousness, the work of the law written in their hearts; however, this work of the law is not the same as the law of God in the heart of the new covenant. It is not the new disposition or nature.

The New Disposition And Regeneration

In the examination of Jeremiah 31 and Ezekiel 36 it was noted that a person receives the new disposition through regeneration. This means that no one can have the new nature apart from regeneration. Since this is so, it would be well to examine somewhat more fully the subject of regeneration and its relationship to the new disposition.

The first thing to be noted about regeneration is the fact that it does not involve a metaphysical change in man. The evidence for this is as follows: once regeneration has been accomplished a person is neither more nor less than a human being.

Secondly, regeneration is concerned primarily with the disposition of man. Berkhof writes:

Regeneration consists in the implanting of the *principle* of the new spiritual life in man, in a radical change of the governing disposition of the soul, which, under the influence of the Holy Spirit, gives birth to a life that moves in a Godward direction. In principle this change affects the whole man.[4]

Thirdly, regeneration involves the placing of a new disposition in man, not a change in the old disposition. That this is so is indicated by the fact that the regenerate person retains his old disposition after receiving the new one (Romans 7:14-25). In addition, the language of Jeremiah 31 implies that the placing of the law of God in the heart involves the placing of something which had not been there before, not the changing of something already there.

Fourthly, regeneration is not a lengthy process; "It is an instantaneous change."[5] Thus, the new disposition is not something that grows or develops in a person over a period of time. It is something that comes to him instantaneously. One moment he is totally without it, but the next moment he has the whole disposition.

Fifthly, regeneration is the same as the new birth or to be born again.[6] Thus, it is correct to say that a person receives the new disposition through the new birth or by being born again (John 3:3). Through his physical birth he receives the old disposition; through his new spiritual birth he receives his new disposition (John 3:6).

Sixthly, since the new disposition is the law of God written in the heart, and since the law is an expression of the holy nature of God, then through regeneration the individual is in a certain sense made partaker of the divine nature. Pink says:

In the new birth we are made partakers of the Divine nature: a principle, a "seed," a life, is communicated to us, which is "born of the Spirit," and therefore "*is* spirit"; being born of the Holy Spirit, it is *holy*. Apart from this Divine and holy nature which is imparted to us at the new birth, it is utterly impossible for any man to generate a spiritual impulse, form a spiritual concept, think a spiritual thought, understand spiritual things, still less engage in spiritual works.[7]

Knudsen states that "the Scriptures, however, describe regeneration as being in another fashion a partaking of the divine nature (II Pet. 1:4)."[8]

Seventhly, regeneration is not something which man can produce; it is entirely a work done by the Holy Spirit in and for man. Berkhof maintains that "the Holy Spirit is the efficient cause of regeneration. This means that the Holy Spirit works directly on the heart of man and changes its spiritual condition."[9]

Pink comments:

If then a man *does* "follow after" that which by nature he cordially dislikes, if he does now love the One he once hated, it is because a miraculous change has taken place within him; a power outside of himself has operated upon him, a nature entirely different from his old one has been imparted to him.[10]

This means that the new disposition cannot be obtained through human effort. It comes solely through the supernatural work of the Holy Spirit.

Eighthly, the ultimate intent and goal of regeneration is that the individual "be transformed into the image of Christ."[11] This is another way of saying that the image of God in man is to be restored to what it was before it became perverted through the fall. Regeneration itself does not produce that restoration, but it makes the restoration possible by giving a person the new disposition.

Commenting on this renewal process and its relationship to regeneration as presented in Titus 3:5-6, Hendriksen states that regeneration "precedes and gives rise to the process of *renewing*. While the latter is a life-long activity, the former is a single act, an instantaneous change."[12]

Alford says that the term "renewal" in Titus 3:5-6 "is used of the gradual renewal of heart and life in the image of God, following upon the new birth."[13]

This means that the new disposition has a job to do: it must play a key role in conforming the regenerated person more and more to the image of God as it originally existed in man.

From all this it has been learned that the new disposition is not a metaphysical substance infused into a person, that it is something new that comes to a person instantaneously through a divine act called "the new birth" or "regeneration," that the new disposition is in a certain sense the divine nature planted in a man, that it cannot be obtained through human effort, and that it has a job to do in conforming a person to the image of God.

5

THE NEW DISPOSITION
AND THE CHRISTIAN

An Important Question and Answer

EARLIER IT WAS NOTED that God has promised to impart the new disposition to members of the nation of Israel in conjunction with His new covenant with that nation. But what can be said of church saints? Do Christians today possess the new disposition? Thankfully, the answer to this question is yes. There are several lines of evidence which indicate that Christians possess the new disposition.

The Regeneration of the Christian

Earlier it was seen that the new disposition comes through the regenerating work of the Holy Spirit. Thus, to be regenerated is also to possess the new disposition.

Titus 3:5-6 teaches that the Christian has been regenerated:

He saved us, not on the basis of deeds which we have done in righteousness, but according to His mercy, by the washing of regeneration and renewing by the Holy Spirit, whom He poured out upon us richly through Jesus Christ our Saviour.

Paul uses the first person plural ("us") in this passage, so it is evident that he regards regeneration as having happened to himself, Titus, and other Christians.

2 Corinthians 3:3

In 2 Corinthians 3:3 Paul tells the Corinthian Christians that they are "a letter of Christ, cared for by us, written not with ink, but with the Spirit of the living God, not on tablets of stone, but on tablets of human hearts." Paul is saying that, as a result of his ministry, Christ wrote something through the Holy Spirit in the hearts of these Christians.

The writing in human hearts is contrasted with the writing upon tablets of stone. In verse 7 Paul's reference to the writing upon stone tablets makes it obvious that he had the old covenant law in mind. Thus, his contrast in verse 3 is between the external old covenant law and what is written internally in believers by God.

As noted earlier, the same contrast was drawn in Jeremiah 31:31-34. There it was the law of God or the new disposition which God promised to write internally upon the heart.

Since both passages have the same contrast, and since it is the new disposition which is written upon the heart in the Jeremiah passage, that which is written upon the heart in the 2 Corinthians passage must also be the new disposition.

2 Peter 1:4

After having told Christians that God's divine power had given to them everything pertaining to life and godliness through their personal, experiential knowledge of Him, Peter writes: "For by these He has granted to us His precious and magnificent promises, in order that by them you might become partakers of *the* divine nature, having escaped the corruption that is in the world by lust."

One thing that must be determined concerning Peter's statement is the meaning of "divine nature." In light of the earlier discussion concerning the meanings of the term "nature," it must be concluded that Peter is not using "divine nature" in the broad sense. He is not referring to that unique combination of attributes which determines that God is deity in contrast with all other kinds of being. Man never partakes of divine nature in that sense, for man can never become deity.

Peter must be using "divine nature" in the narrow sense; he must be referring to the holy disposition of God. Peter is saying that Christians partake of the divine nature in the sense that they receive a disposition which is an expression of the holy nature of God.

The context indicates that Peter is using "divine nature" in the narrow sense. In the preceding verse he talks about God having granted to Christians "everything pertaining to life and godliness." Certainly the new disposition is one key thing necessary for living a godly life. In addition, in verse 5 Peter talks about Christians having moral excellence. Thus, the entire context is concerned with what issues in a godly, moral life, not with what makes one deity.

Concerning Peter's usage of "divine nature," Demarest writes:

To partake of *the* divine nature is in itself impossible; for the distinction between God and intelligent beings, created and renewed by Him, is infinite and impassable, and can never, from the very nature of the thing, be annihilated. If it could be, Pantheism would be true. But, to confound the Creator and the creature, and to make them all one and the same, is madness and blasphemy. "Nature," then, as here used by the apostle, cannot mean essence or substance, but disposition, moral qualities. And *to become partakers of a divine nature,* means to become partakers of a disposition like that of God. . . . "Partakers of His holiness," Hebrews 12:10, and "partakers of a divine nature," are identical in signification.[1]

In light of 2 Peter 1:4 it can be concluded that Christians do have the new disposition which is an expression of the holy nature of God.

Romans 7:22

The Different Views

In Romans 7:14-25 Paul describes a great spiritual struggle which he experienced sometime during his life. Scholars
have differed concerning the nature of this struggle. Some
have argued that Paul describes his unregenerate experience
when he lived as a Pharisee under the old covenant law.[2]
Others have been convinced that Paul describes an experience which he had as a regenerate man.[3]

A few scholars hold to a view which is a combination of
the unregenerate and regenerate views. According to them
Romans 7:14-25 is:

a description of the distressing experience of any morally earnest
man, whether Christian or not, who attempts to live up to the
commands of God "on his own" . . . without that constant reliance
upon the uninterrupted supply of the resources of God, which is
characteristic of the mature Christian.[4]

The author is convinced of the regenerate view for reasons that will be stated.[5]

Arguments for the Regenerate View

The view which says that Paul in Romans 7:14-25 describes an experience which he had as a regenerate man has
a number of arguments in its favor. Firstly, in Romans 7:7-13,
where scholars agree that Paul is describing his condition as
an unregenerate man, Paul uses nonpresent tense verbs. But
in 7:14-25 he switches to using all present tense verbs. Why
would Paul switch tenses save for the purpose of indicating
that in the latter passage he is relating an experience from his
present regenerate state?[6]

Secondly, what Paul writes in Romans 7:14-25 is not

consistent with what he wrote of the unregenerate in Romans 1:18—3:20. In Romans 7 Paul gives hearty approval to the holy law of God, but in Romans 1:18—3:20 the unregenerate give hearty approval to those who sin. In Romans 7 Paul wills to do the revealed will of God, but in Romans 1 the unregenerate willfully reject the revelation of God.[7]

Thirdly, it is highly unlikely that an unregenerate person would declare himself to be flesh, sold under sin (Romans 7:14). The unsaved usually are unaware of their bondage to sin.

Fourthly, only the regenerate truly hate sin (Romans 7:15).

Fifthly, an unsaved person does not have the spiritual perception necessary to distinguish between his inner self and his sinful disposition (Romans 7:17).

Sixthly, the unbeliever does not delight in the law of God in the inner man (Romans 7:22) and serve it with his mind (7:25). According to Romans 8:7 and Colossians 1:21, the unregenerate mind is hostile toward God and His law.[8]

Seventhly, Romans 7:14-25 cannot be describing an unsaved person under conviction for sin, for Paul "is crying for deliverance—not from sin's guilt and penalty, but from its power. Not for forgiveness of sins, but help against indwelling sin. This man is exercised, not about the day of judgment, but about a condition of bondage to that which he hates."[9]

Eighthly, the will of the unregenerate person is united in agreement with the sinful disposition, but in Romans 7:14-25 Paul's will is in opposition to the sinful disposition.[10]

Ninthly, if Paul is not speaking of a regenerate experience in Romans 7:14-25, then his argument which begins with Romans 6:14 and extends into Romans 8 is incomplete. Paul's purpose beginning with 6:14 is to contrast the principles of law and grace by demonstrating the superiority of grace over the old covenant law as the means of sanctification. Unless Paul demonstrates the failure of the old covenant law as the means of sanctification, his argument is incomplete. Only the regenerate view allows for this demonstration.[11]

The Statement in Romans 7:22

Having concluded that Paul is speaking of a regenerate experience in Romans 7:14-25, attention is now focused upon Paul's statement in Romans 7:22: "For I joyfully concur with the law of God in the inner man." The word translated "I joyfully concur" is very strong. It is much stronger in meaning than the word translated "I agree with" in verse sixteen.[12] "It is the agreement of moral sympathy."[13]

Murray states it this way: "And this delight is not peripheral but belongs to that which is deepest and inmost in his moral and spiritual being."[14] It is for this reason that Paul declares that the location of his delight in the law of God is in the inner man.

Behm declares that that which Paul calls the inner man corresponds to that which the Old Testament calls the heart.[15] This equation of the inner man with the heart appears to be correct, for Paul in Romans 7 indicates that the inner man is the moral center of man, and Christ in Mark 7:20-23 teaches that the heart is the moral center of man. Thus, when Paul says that he joyfully concurs with the law of God in the inner man, it is the same as saying that he joyfully concurs with the law of God in the heart.

Before regeneration Paul was a Pharisee in his relationship to the law of God (Philippians 3:5). A major characteristic of the Pharisees was this: they delighted in the law of God according to the outer man. That this was so is evidenced by what Jesus said to them in Matthew 23:25-28:

Woe to you, scribes and Pharisees, hypocrites! For you clean the outside of the cup and of the dish, but inside they are full of robbery and self-indulgence. You blind Pharisee, first clean the inside of the cup and of the dish, so that the outside of it may become clean also. Woe to you, scribes and Pharisees, hypocrites! For you are like whitewashed tombs which on the outside appear beautiful, but inside they are full of dead men's bones and all uncleanness. Even so you too outwardly appear righteous to men, but inwardly you are full of hypocrisy and lawlessness.

It was because the Pharisees emphasized only external conformity to the law of God that Jesus said in the Sermon on the Mount: "For I say to you, that unless your righteousness surpasses *that* of the scribes and Pharisees, you shall not enter the kingdom of heaven" (Matthew 5:20). After saying this, Jesus illustrated what He meant by contrasting the teaching of the Pharisees with the real demand of the law. The Pharisees emphasized conformity of outward act to the law, but the law demanded conformity of inward disposition. Mere outward conformity without a genuine, holy, inner disposition was not sufficient to make one a member of God's kingdom. This, then, was Jesus' way of saying that a person must have the new disposition in the inner man.

Thus, as an unregenerate Pharisee, Paul delighted in the law of God after the outer man, but now that he has become a Christian he delights in it in the inner man. The reason for the drastic change is this: through regeneration he has received the new disposition, the law of God in the heart.

Conclusion

This chapter has demonstrated the fact that Christians or church saints do possess the new disposition or nature.

6

THE BACKGROUND OF THE STRUGGLE
OF THE CHRISTIAN

The Necessary Examination

NOW THAT IT HAS BEEN DEMONSTRATED that all Christians have the law of God written in their hearts, it is necessary to deal with the work of the new disposition. What does it do for the Christian in daily living? Does it have limitations? Paul answers these questions in Romans 7:14-25 where, as seen earlier, he describes part of his own Christian experience. In order to understand the experience he describes there, it is necessary to first examine the context preceding that passage.

Preliminary Considerations Concerning the Context

The Meaning of the Word "Sin"

Paul uses the term "sin" a total of twenty-five times in Romans 6:1—7:13. One of these usages (6:15) refers to an act of sin. Most, if not all, of the other twenty-four usages, seem to refer to the sinful disposition or nature.[1]

There are several reasons for this conclusion. Firstly, in Romans 6:12-13 Paul pictures sin as a reigning monarch to whom human subjects offer their bodies to fulfill the monarch's commanded acts. Thus, Paul is regarding sin, not as an act, but as a governing disposition which demands acts.

Secondly, in Romans 6:6,14,17,20 Paul pictures sin as a master who orders slaves to act as the master desires. Again, Paul is regarding sin, not as an act, but as the thing which governs and orders acts.

Thirdly, in 7:7-8 Paul declares that sin produced coveting (lust) of every kind in him. According to James 1:14-15 lust in turn gives birth to an act of sin. The joining of these passages indicates that Paul is not talking about an act of sin. Instead, he refers to the sinful disposition which prompts the chain reaction which produces the act of sin.

Earlier it was noted that, since fallen man's disposition is one of enmity against God, it is correct to call that disposition "sin."

The Personification of Sin

As Paul deals with the sinful disposition under the title of "sin" in Romans 6—7, he personifies it repeatedly. This personification has been recognized by numerous scholars. For example, Hamilton says that "Paul calls this personified corrupt nature 'sin.' "[2]

The fact that Paul does personify sin does not mean that he regards the sin nature as being a person instead of a governing disposition. Instead, it means that he simply uses a figure of speech to make a difficult spiritual truth more understandable to his readers. Thus, in Romans 6:19, where Paul deals with one aspect of the personification (the master—slave relationship), he states that he is speaking in "human terms" because of the weakness of his readers' flesh.

Concerning Paul's statement Murray writes: "The dullness of our understanding makes it necessary that we be taught the truth in figures drawn from the sphere of our human relations."[3]

As the author of this study deals with the sinful and new dispositions, he too will use terms of personification. There is little alternative to this procedure, for in his attempt to explain accurately what Paul is teaching the author must remain faithful to the figures of speech which Paul uses. The reader must not interpret the author's use of personification as meaning that he regards the sin and new natures as being persons instead of dispositions.

The Master—Slave Analogy

As Paul attempts to explain the relationship of human beings to sin and God, the instrument that he uses most frequently is the analogy of the master—slave relationship. In Romans 6:6,16-20,22 he asserts that people are slaves either to sin, impurity, and lawlessness or to righteousness, obedience, and God. In Romans 6:14 he refers to sin as a master.

Murray states concerning Paul's teaching:

He describes the condition of unbelievers as slavery to sin and he also describes the state of believers as bondservice to righteousness. The institution of slavery, well-known to his readers, is the medium through which he expresses the truth. In using this analogy drawn from the sphere of human relations he speaks after the manner of men.[4]

Since Paul uses the analogy of the master—slave relationship, it is necessary to examine what the terms "master" and "slave" meant in his day in order to understand what he is teaching.

The key idea in the word that Paul uses for "master" is that of a legal position of authority.[5] Thus, when Paul speaks of a master in Romans 6, he is thinking of one who holds a legal position of authority over a slave. A legal position of authority gives the master the right to dominate or control every aspect of the slave's total being.

In Paul's day the key idea in the word that he uses for "slave" was this: the will of the slave is to be subject to the will of the master.[6] "Alongside the will and commission of the [master] there is no place for one's own will or initiative."[7] Thus, when Paul speaks of a slave in Romans 6, he is thinking of one who has a position of subjection in which his will is not to be self-governing. This means that the slave is obligated to render complete obedience to the dictates of his master.

The Slavery of the Unregenerate Man

In Romans 6:6,16-20 Paul teaches that the unregenerate man exists in a master—slave relationship with his sinful disposition. As he reminds the Roman Christians of what they were before they became saved, he says: "You were slaves of sin" (Romans 6:17,20). The sinful disposition gained the legal position of master over man as a result of man voluntarily committing himself to the service of sin at the time of the fall (Romans 6:16). Fallen man came into the subject position of a slave.

The key ideas in the terms "master" and "slave" which were noted earlier reveal several factors involved in this master—slave relationship. Firstly, as a master the sinful disposition holds the legal position of authority over the unregenerate man. By virtue of this position it has the right to dominate and control every aspect of the unregenerate man's total being, including his body, mind, and will. As noted before, this control of every part of fallen man's total nature by his sin nature is called "total depravity."

Secondly, because unregenerate man holds the position of slave under his sinful disposition, his will does not have the right to be self-governing. This means that unsaved man is obligated to render complete obedience to the dictates of the sinful disposition. He has no choice but to do what it prompts him to do.

Because, as seen earlier, man became confirmed in his sinful disposition through the fall, the position of master gained by that disposition is a lasting one. Unregenerate man is so thoroughly locked into the master—slave relationship with the sin nature that he is held in his position of slave as long as he lives in the unregenerate state. The only thing that can end this master—slave relationship is death. Either the sinful disposition or the unregenerate man must die.

The Death of the Unregenerate Man

In Romans 6:1-13 Paul indicates that when an unregenerate man becomes a Christian he is identified with Jesus Christ. This involves identification with the death, burial, and resurrection of Christ. Concerning the first aspect of identification, Paul teaches that there is some sense in which the unregenerate man actually dies with Christ when that person becomes a Christian. One way in which Paul expresses this truth is as follows: "Knowing this, that our old man was crucified with *Him*" (Romans 6:6, a literal translation).

The Meaning of "Old Man"

Scholars disagree as to what Paul means by "old man." Some take the position that by "old man" Paul means the sinful disposition or old nature. For example, Erdman claims that Paul is teaching that "our old dispositions and appetites and evil desires have been put to death."[8] According to this view, in Romans 6:1-13 Paul is asserting that the Christian's sinful disposition has been crucified or has died with Christ.

Other scholars are convinced that by "old man" Paul means the unregenerate man or the person in his unregenerate state. Wuest says that "the old man here refers to that person the believer was before he was saved, totally depraved, unregenerate, lacking the life of God."[9] According to this view, then, Paul is teaching that the unregenerate man or person has been crucified or has died with Christ.

The author is convinced of the second view for several

reasons. Firstly, the whole context of Romans 6:1-13 talks about persons, not dispositions, having died. In Romans 6:2,8 Paul says that "we" died; in verse 7 he says that "he" died. A disposition is only one aspect of a person; it cannot be said that in reality it is a person.

Secondly, in Romans 6:7 Paul draws a distinction between the person who died and the sinful disposition. He declares that the person who died is freed from the sinful disposition. He thereby makes it clear that it is the person, not the disposition, that died.

Thirdly, the view that says that it is the sinful disposition that died with Christ distorts the concept of identification with Christ's death taught in this passage. When Christ died it was a person, not just a disposition, that died. Christ became a human being so that He could die as the substitute for human persons, not as the substitute for a sinful disposition.

Fourthly, when Paul applies his teaching (Romans 6:11), he exhorts Christians to reckon *themselves* to be dead. He does not tell them to reckon their sinful dispositions to be dead. Certainly Paul would have exhorted the latter if their dispositions had been crucified.

Fifthly, in Romans 6:2,11 Paul declares that the believer has died to sin. He does not say that sin has died to the believer.

Sixthly, if the sinful disposition has been crucified with Christ, then that disposition is dead in the Christian. This would mean that the Christian has no struggle with sin. But Romans 7:14-25 indicates that the Christian does have a struggle with sin. In fact, Romans 7:14-25 and Galatians 5 teach that the sinful disposition is very much alive and active in the Christian.

Seventhly, in a parallel passage (Galatians 2:20) Paul declares that it was he who was crucified with Christ. He does not say that his sinful disposition was crucified.

It should be concluded, then, that the *"old man" is the*

unregenerate man or the human person in his unregenerate state. As an old man, the unsaved person holds the position of slave under his sinful disposition.

In light of this meaning of "old man," when Paul says that our old man was crucified with Christ, he is teaching that there is some sense in which the unregenerate person actually dies when he becomes a Christian.

The Nature of the Death

This teaching of Paul prompts an important question. In what sense does an unregenerate person die with Christ when he becomes a Christian? Certainly he does not die physically, for the person continues to have the same body after regeneration as before regeneration. Again, he does not die metaphysically, for he continues to be the same person metaphysically after the new birth as before the new birth. He continues to have the same personal name, background, parents, place of employment, and residence. The fact that Paul uses the terms "you" and "we" when describing the former unregenerate condition of himself and other Christians (Ephesians 2:1-7) indicates that he regards believers as being the same persons metaphysically that they were in their unregenerate state.

The unsaved person dies with Christ in the sense that he ceases to be an unregenerate man. Before regeneration he was an "old man," an unregenerate man. However, at the moment of the new birth he ceases to be an "old man."

A Significant Change

Although the Christian remains the same person metaphysically that he was while unregenerate, the Scriptures do regard him as a different person in some sense. The Christian is "a new creature" (2 Corinthians 5:17), he is in the state of "a new creation" (Galatians 6:15) and is said to have been "created in Christ Jesus" (Ephesians 2:10). The fact that Christians are called "newborn babes" (1 Peter 2:2) indicates that they are regarded as new persons. The use of the terms "old man" and "new man" (Colossians 3:9-10) to describe the individual in his unregenerate and regenerate states shows that there is some sense in which the individual is regarded as one person in his unregenerate state but as another person in his regenerate state.

The author is convinced that it is in the spiritual sense that the Scriptures regard the Christian as being a different person. The individual is one person spiritually in his unregenerate state but is another person spiritually in his regenerate state. In his unregenerate state he is an "old man" who is characterized by rebellion against the rule of God. In his regenerate state he is a "new man" who is favorably disposed toward the rule of God.

Although the Christian was one person *spiritually* in his unregenerate state and is another person *spiritually* in his regenerate state, he is still the same person *metaphysically* in his regenerate state that he was in his unregenerate state. The recognition of this distinction between the spiritual and metaphysical senses of the person helps in the understanding of Galatians 2:20. In that passage Paul indicates that there is a sense in which he as a person was crucified and no longer lives, but there is also a sense in which he as a person does still live. It would appear that what Paul means is this: the person that he was spiritually while in the unregenerate state has been crucified with Christ and no longer lives, but the person that he was metaphysically before co-crucifixion still continues to live. On the one hand he is no longer the man who hated Jesus Christ, persecuted Christians, and exulted in his self-righteousness; but on the other hand he is still the same man who was born in Tarsus, studied under Gamaliel, and possessed Roman citizenship by birth (Acts 22:3-28).

The Finality of the Death

Scholars agree that in Romans 6:1-13 Paul is talking about a death which is related somehow to Christians. They disagree, however, concerning the finality of this death in relationship to Christians. Some see the crucifixion of Romans 6:6 as a lifelong agonizing process of the Christian putting to death his sinful disposition or his love for sin.[10] Others, who see this death as a continuing process of the believer dying to self and the world, refer to 1 Corinthians 15:31 where Paul says: "I die daily."[11]

In contrast with those who see the death of Romans 6 as an incomplete, continuing process, several scholars believe it is a once-for-all death which was completed for the Christian in the past.[12]

The author is convinced that the evidence is in favor of the latter view. Firstly, the idea of a continuous, incomplete process of dying in this passage ruins the concept of identification with the death of Christ which is taught in the context. According to Romans 6:10, Christ's death was once-for-all in the past. Since this is so, any other kind of death in this passage makes true identification with the death of Christ impossible.

Secondly, in Romans 6:11 Paul exhorts Christians to consider themselves to be dead to sin. He does not exhort them to consider themselves to be dying to sin. The language implies that they are to reckon themselves as being already in a fixed state of death, not in a continuing process of dying.

Thirdly, Paul's question in Romans 6:2: "How shall we who died to sin still live in it?" makes no sense if the death in question is not a past, completed fact. For the person who is only in the process of dying to sin, it is still possible to live in sin. Only for the person who has terminated his relationship to sin by a completed death is it possible to avoid continuing in sin.

This evidence is not annulled by Paul's "I die daily"

statement in 1 Corinthians 15:31. The context of this statement indicates that Paul is not talking about a process by
which he is continually dying to sin and the world. In verse
30 he talks about being "in danger every hour." In verse 32
he refers to a fight that threatened his physical life. In light
of these expressions, the statement "I die daily" would appear to mean that either Paul's life was in constant jeopardy
or that he was continually ready to lay down his life for Christ
if need be.[13] Thus, Paul is talking about the prospect of physical death, not some aspect of progressive sanctification.

It should be concluded then that the co-crucifixion with
Christ taught in Romans 6:1-13 is a once-for-all, completed,
past event for the Christian. It is not in the process of happen-
ing.

The Reference of the Death

In Romans 6:2 Paul declares that the Christian has died
with reference to sin. When interpreting this statement two
things should be kept in mind. Firstly, as noted earlier, in this
context the term "sin" refers to the sinful disposition. Secondly, the case that Paul uses for the noun translated "to sin" is
primarily a case of personal relations even when applied to
things.[14] In light of these two things Paul is saying that the
Christian has died with reference to the personal relationship
which he had with his sinful disposition while in the unregenerate state.

Since in Romans 6 the Christian's death with Christ is
once-for-all and completed, and since the unregenerate person's relationship with his sinful disposition is a master—
slave relationship, it can be concluded that Paul is teaching
the following: through his death with Christ the person loses
completely and once-for-all the master—slave relationship
which he had with his sinful disposition while in the unregenerate state; the sinful disposition loses completely and forever
its legal position of master over the person; and the person

loses completely and forever his position of slave under his sinful disposition.

The First Purpose of the Death

In Romans 6:6 Paul declares that one purpose for the old man's crucifixion with Christ is "that our body of sin might be done away with."

Scholars have proposed four different interpretations of the expression "body of sin." Firstly, some believe that it refers to the sin nature or disposition.[15] Secondly, a few claim that by "body of sin" Paul means all sin in one mass considered figuratively as a body.[16] In other words, it is the sum total of all sinful acts. Thirdly, others see the "body of sin" as the person who sins.[17,18] Fourthly, a number of scholars regard the "body of sin" as the physical body of the unregenerate man characterized as an instrument of service to the sinful disposition. Gifford states this view: "This is the body of the old man that was crucified, that is to say, it is the natural body in its old condition, as the servant of sin."[19]

Those who hold to the fourth view are careful to assert what they do not mean by their view. They do not mean that the physical body by itself is sinful or the source of sin.[20] They are right in this, for Adam before the fall had a body and yet was without sin, and Jesus Christ had a human body and also was without sin (Hebrews 4:15). Thus, according to this view, the body of the unregenerate man is not the source of sin; instead it serves as the instrument of the sinful disposition. In this sense the human body is the "body of sin."

The author is convinced that this last view is correct for several reasons. Firstly, this view is consistent with the meaning which Paul attaches to the term "body" every other time he uses that term in this context. He calls the body "your mortal body" (Romans 6:12; 8:11), and he talks of "the members of your body" being presented as instruments to sin (6:13). In Romans 7:23 Paul mentions a law which operates in "the members of my body." In Romans 8:10 he contrasts body with spirit. In Romans 8:23 he talks about the future redemption of the body. These references indicate that in the context of Romans 6:6 Paul's concept of body is that of the natural human body.

Secondly, this view is consistent with the master—slave analogy which Paul uses in Romans 6. Just as the slave's body is ruled by the master, so the unregenerate man's body is ruled by his master, the sinful disposition.

Thirdly, this view is consistent with the case of the word "sin" in the expression "body of sin." Moule specifically declares that in Romans 6:6 this case has a strong adjectival use. As a result, the expression "body of sin" has the force of "sin-possessed body."[21] It refers to the body that is possessed or controlled by the sinful disposition.

What did Paul mean when he said that the body of sin might be "done away with"? The literal meaning of the expression "done away with" is "to put out of business" or "to dissolve business relationships."[22] Paul uses the same verb again in Romans 7:2 and 7:6. In both instances he uses it to express release from a relationship to law. In light of this, it would appear that in this context Paul uses the verb to express the termination of a relationship.

In light of the meanings of "body of sin" and "done away with" the following conclusion can be drawn: the first purpose of death with Christ is the termination of the relationship which exists between the unregenerate man's physical body and his sinful disposition. The unregenerate man's physical body is the servant of his sinful disposition. It is a sin-controlled body. It is obligated to function as an instrument of sin. When the unregenerate man dies with Christ his physical body terminates its former relationship with the sinful disposition. No longer is it the servant of the sinful disposition. No longer is it obligated to function as an instrument of sin. It ceases to be the "body of sin."

The termination of this relationship is impossible unless

the master—slave relationship between the sinful disposition and the person who has the body also terminates. Thus, the first purpose of death with Christ implies that, when the person dies with Christ, his sinful disposition loses its position of master over him, and he loses his position of slave to that disposition.

The Second Purpose of the Death

Paul continues Romans 6:6 by stating that the second purpose for the old man's crucifixion with Christ is "that we should no longer be slaves to sin."

The term "no longer" implies that at one time Paul and his readers had been slaves to their sinful dispositions, but they died with Christ for the purpose of not continuing any longer in that relationship.

The expression "be slaves" refers to "one that is in a permanent relation of servitude to another, his will altogether swallowed up in the will of the other."[23]

The second purpose, then, for the unregenerate person's death with Christ is the permanent termination of the relationship of slavery to his sinful disposition into which he was bound for life.

The Third Purpose of the Death

In Romans 6:4 Paul states that the third purpose for the unregenerate man's death with Christ is "in order that . . . we too might walk in newness of life." Verse 5 explains why this walk in newness of life is possible. The person who is united with Christ in His death is also united with Him in His resurrection. Paul is teaching that there is some sense in which a person actually experiences resurrection with Christ when that person becomes a Christian.

What is the nature of this resurrection which the person experiences through union with Christ? Certainly the person is not resurrected physically at the moment he becomes a Christian, for he did not die physically before becoming a Christian. Again, he is not resurrected metaphysically, for he is the same person metaphysically after the new birth as before the new birth. He continues to have the same personal name, background, parents, place of employment, and residence.

The person who believes in Christ is resurrected in the sense that he becomes a regenerate person, the "new man," with the new disposition and the Holy Spirit within him. Thus, it is a spiritual resurrection. The new disposition and Holy Spirit give him a newness of life which produces a new walk or way of life. This will be treated more fully as the study progresses.

Paul clearly indicates that the new walk is to be characterized by righteousness (Romans 6:13,19). Such a righteous walk would be impossible if the Christian were to continue in the master—slave relationship with his sinful disposition after the new birth. Thus, the third purpose of death with Christ implies that when the person dies with Christ his sinful disposition loses its position of master over him, and he loses his position of slave to that disposition.

The Result of the Death

In Romans 6:7 Paul states the result of death with Christ: the person who has died "is freed from sin." In other words, the person is freed from his sinful disposition or nature.

This statement of Paul prompts an important question. In what sense is the person who has died with Christ freed from his sinful disposition? At least four different answers to this question have been proposed. Firstly, some say that, when the person dies with Christ, he is freed from the presence of his sinful disposition. This would mean that the Christian has no sinful disposition. This view must be rejected, for it is contrary to what other Scriptures teach. Passages such as

Romans 7:14-25 clearly indicate that the sinful disposition is still present and active within the believer.

Secondly, others claim that the person who has died with Christ is freed from the power or influence of sin.[24] The sinful disposition is with the Christian, but it cannot exert influence in his life anymore. This view also runs contrary to Romans 7:14-25 which demonstrates that the sinful disposition can exert power or influence in the life of the Christian.

Thirdly, a number of scholars believe that Romans 6:7 is teaching that, when a person dies with Christ, God judicially declares him to be free from the guilt, penalty, and judgment of sin.[25] They base this view upon the fact that the word translated "freed" is a legal term.[26]

Proponents of this third view are correct when they point out that Paul normally uses the word translated "freed" in the sense of God judicially declaring a person free from the guilt, penalty, and judgment of sin. In spite of this normal usage, however, the author rejects this third view for several reasons.

Firstly, in the section covered by Romans 6—8 Paul deals with sanctification, not justification in the normal sense. In Romans 6:1-2 he talks about continuing or living in the sphere of sin. In verse 12 he mentions sin reigning in the mortal body and persons rendering obedience to its lusts. In Romans 7:14-25 he talks about practicing evil rather than good, and in Romans 8:1-4 he refers to the Christian's walk. In all these statements Paul is referring to a manner of living, not to guilt, penalty, and judgment, or to justification from these things.

Secondly, the third view has the Christian freed merely from the consequences of sin, but Paul states that the Christian is freed from sin itself.

Thirdly, this third view does not fit the master—slave analogy which Paul uses in the context. Paul presents the analogy of a slave rendering obedient service to his master and of that slave being freed from the same master. Although it makes sense to think of a person being freed from guilt, penalty, and judgment, it does not make sense to think of a person rendering obedient service to these things.

The fourth view, maintained by several scholars, asserts that the person who has died with Christ has been freed from the sinful disposition itself in the sense that he has lost it as his master. The sinful disposition is still with the person, but it no longer holds its legal position of master over him.[27]

Scholars who hold this view recognize that it has Paul using the term translated "freed" in a different sense from the way that he normally uses it. It has him using it for release from a relationship formerly existing with the sinful disposition.

These same scholars hasten to point out two things concerning this seemingly unusual use of the term. Firstly, this use did appear in ancient literature; therefore it was known in Paul's day.[28] Secondly, even with this use the term continues to maintain its legal sense. Sanday and Headlam declare: "The idea is that of a master claiming legal possession of a slave: proof being put in that the slave is dead, the verdict must needs be that the claims of law are satisfied and that he is no longer answerable; sin loses its suit."[29]

The author accepts this fourth view as the correct one for several reasons. Firstly, this view fits best with the master—slave analogy which Paul uses in this context. As noted earlier, the key idea in the word for "master" in Romans 6:14 is that of a legal position of authority. In Paul's day a master held a legal position of authority over a slave. This gave the master the right to control every aspect of the slave's total being. The slave was obligated to render complete obedience to the dictates of his master. This legal master—slave relationship was terminated by the death of the slave.

By analogy Paul is teaching that the sinful disposition holds the legal position of master over the unregenerate man, and the unregenerate man holds the position of slave under his sinful disposition. This gives the sinful disposition the right to control every aspect of the unregenerate man's total being. The unregenerate man is obligated to render complete obedience to the dictates of his sinful disposition. This master—slave relationship is terminated by the unregenerate man's death with Christ. The person who dies with Christ is freed from his sinful disposition in the sense that it loses its legal position of master over him. Thus, death with Christ results in legal freedom from a legal master—slave relationship.

Secondly, the fourth view gives Romans 6:7 the meaning which most logically explains the last clause of Romans 6:6: "that we should no longer be slaves to sin." Since Paul begins verse seven with the word "for," it seems apparent that he is explaining why the person who dies with Christ ceases to be a slave to his sinful disposition. The reason is this: he who has died has been freed from his sinful disposition in the sense that he has lost it as his master. Death has terminated that master—slave relationship.

Thirdly, this view fits best with Romans 6:17-22 where Paul teaches that in the past his readers had been slaves of their sinful dispositions, but now they have been freed and have become slaves of righteousness. The very fact that Paul's readers have a new master implies that their sinful dispositions have ceased being their master.

The Responsibilities of the Christian

In Romans 6:11-13 Paul teaches that the Christian has certain responsibilities in light of his freedom from the sinful disposition and resurrection with Christ.

The First Responsibility

The slaveholder who has lost his position of master over a slave may try to continue dominating his former slave. In spite of the fact that he has no legal right to do this, the former master will succeed in his attempt unless his former

The New Nature

slave reckons on the fact that his previous relationship with this master has been terminated. Only if he takes this fact into account will the former slave recognize that he is no longer obligated to obey this man and thereby refuse to render service to him.

By analogy the sinful disposition, after it has lost its position of master over the person who has died with Christ, tries to continue dominating its former slave. In spite of the fact that it has no right to do this, the sinful disposition succeeds in its attempt unless the regenerate person reckons on the fact that his former master—slave relationship with this disposition has been terminated as a result of his death with Christ. Only if the regenerate man takes this fact into account will he recognize that he is no longer obligated to obey the sinful disposition and thereby refuse to render service to it.

Because this is true, in Romans 6:11 Paul commands the Christian to reckon himself to be dead to his sinful disposition. Paul expresses this command in the present tense. Since, as noted before, the sinful disposition continues with the Christian, Paul no doubt intends the present tense to be taken in the continual sense: "Keep on considering yourselves to be dead to sin."

The first responsibility of the Christian, then, is that every time the sinful disposition tries to control the Christian to commit sin he should remember the fact that that disposition is no longer his master. It lost that position forever when the person died with Christ. Thus, the Christian should recognize that he is no longer obligated to obey his sinful disposition. He now has a choice. He should refuse to render service to it.

The Second Responsibility

The second responsibility of the Christian is that he is to reckon himself "alive to God in Christ Jesus" (Romans 6:11).

It appears that this responsibility is associated with the truth that the Christian has been resurrected spiritually with Christ to be a regenerate man with the new disposition and Holy Spirit within him (verses 4-5). When he was an "old man" the person existed in a unique personal relationship with his sinful disposition, and his life was characterized by that relationship. Now that he is a "new man" the person is alive with reference to God. He lives in a unique personal relationship with God, and he has tremendous potential to live a new kind of life. In light of this truth Paul is commanding the Christian to reckon on the fact that he has been made spiritually alive with reference to God.

Since this command is expressed with the same verb as the previous command, it too is to be understood in the continual sense: "Keep on considering yourselves to be alive to God in Christ Jesus." The second responsibility of the Christian, then, is that every time the sinful disposition tries to control the Christian to commit sin, he should remember the fact that he now lives in a unique personal relationship with God; therefore, his life is to be characterized by that relationship.

The Third Responsibility

The Christian's third responsibility is to "not let sin reign in your mortal body that you should obey its lusts" (Romans 6:12). When the person was unregenerate, his sinful disposition reigned like a king over his physical body, making it a "body of sin." It used his body as an instrument to perform its evil deeds. Because the person's death with Christ ended his master—slave relationship with his sinful disposition and because his resurrection with Christ placed him in a vital personal relationship with God, the believer is to keep on (present tense) refusing to allow his sinful disposition to use his body as an instrument. He is to say no every time the sinful disposition stirs up lusts and tries to dominate his body.

The Fourth Responsibility

The fourth responsibility of the regenerate man is to "not go on presenting the members of your body to sin as instruments of unrighteousness" (Romans 6:13). Whereas the previous responsibility dealt with the proper use of the entire body, this one deals with the proper use of individual members of that body. Romans 6:19 indicates that Paul's readers, while in their former position of slavery, had put the individual members of their bodies at the disposal of their sinful dispositions to be used as tools for the performance of evil deeds. Eyes, ears, tongues, hands, feet, and sexual members had been used in ways offensive to God. But now that their sinful dispositions had lost the position of master over them they were not to put the members of their bodies at the disposal of those dispositions again. Thus, the Christian is to say no to the sinful disposition every time it tries to use an individual member of his body.

The Fifth Responsibility

The fifth responsibility presented by Paul is to "present yourselves to God as those alive from the dead" (Romans 6:13). In Romans 6:16 Paul declares that when one person presents himself to another person to be his obedient slave, he thereby becomes the other person's slave. In light of this declaration, in the fifth responsibility Paul commands the Christian to present his total being to God to be God's slave. Now that the person has been freed from the sinful disposition as master, he is to take God as his new Lord and Master.

This time Paul does not use the present tense as he did in the first four responsibilities. This would seem to indicate that the Christian's presentation of himself to be God's slave is a once-for-all transaction, not something that needs to be repeated continually. Once the Christian makes that commitment, he is God's slave forever. Each day of his life is to be lived in accord with that commitment.

The Sixth Responsibility

For the sixth responsibility Paul says to "present your members as instruments of righteousness to God" (Romans 6:13). Whereas the fifth responsibility commanded the Christian to present his total being to God, this responsibility commands him to present the individual members of his body to God to be used as instruments of righteousness. Since Paul uses the same verb for the fifth and sixth responsibilities, it would appear that this presentation is also a once-for-all transaction. Once-for-all the believer is to dedicate each individual member of his body to God to be used in ways pleasing to God. The eyes, ears, tongue, hands, feet, and sexual members are to be presented in such a way that they will not be used contrary to the character and will of God, the new Master.

The Release From Law

The Declaration of Release from Law

Up to this point Paul has emphasized one major result of a person's death with Christ—release from the sinful disposition as master. Now in Romans 6:14 he declares a second major result of death with Christ—release from law.

Paul begins verse fourteen: "Sin shall not be master over you." What Paul is teaching through this statement is that it is a certain fact of reality that at no time in the future will the sinful disposition ever hold the position of master again over the person who has died with Christ.

Paul continues in Romans 6:14 by giving the reason for his first statement. The person who has died with Christ will never have the sinful disposition as master again because that person is "not under law, but under grace."

Several things should be noted concerning this declaration of release from law. Firstly, Paul is drawing a contrast between two positions: the position of being under law and the position of being under grace.[30] His use of the word "under" for both positions indicates that both involve subjection to some governing principle.[31] Those who are "under" law are in the position of subjection to law as a governing principle. Those who are "under" grace are in the position of subjection to grace as a governing principle.

Secondly, Paul is indicating that there is some relationship between being under law as a governing principle and having the sinful disposition as master. He will develop this truth further in Romans 7.

Thirdly, Paul is teaching that there is some relationship between being under grace as a governing principle and not having the sinful disposition as master. As a governing principle for daily living, grace is able to do what external law cannot do: release a person from mastery by his sinful disposition. Paul will develop this truth further in Romans 7 and 8.

Fourthly, Paul is declaring that Christians are not under any external law as a means of sanctification. The word "the" is missing before the word "law"; therefore, Paul is not referring to any specific law system. He is teaching that no external law will set a person free from mastery by his sinful disposition. Although Paul is not referring to any specific law system in Romans 6:14, he does refer specifically to the old covenant law system in Romans 7:4-7 where he explains his statement in 6:14. This indicates that he regards the old covenant law as being part of the external law referred to in 6:14. Thus, in 6:14 Paul is teaching that Christians are not under any external law, not even the old covenant law, as a means of sanctification.

The author concludes that in Romans 6:14 Paul is teaching that the reason Christians will never again have the sinful disposition as master over them is that Christians are not under any external law (including the old covenant law) as a governing principle for sanctification. Instead, they are under grace for sanctification.

An Illustration of Release from Law

Scholars who deal with the antecedent of Romans 7 are convinced that Romans 6:14 is that antecedent.[32] In Romans 7:1-3 Paul uses the illustration of marriage to illustrate his statement that sin shall not be master over the Christian, for the Christian is not under law but under grace (6:14).

In the illustration Paul states that a woman is bound by law to her husband as long as he lives. That bondage is abolished by death. If the woman's husband dies, she is released from the law that bound her to her husband and is free to be married to another husband.

The Application of the Illustration

Interpretations of the wife and husband. In the application (Romans 7:4-6) of the illustration, Paul indicates that the woman of the illustration represents an individual person (verse 4). Many scholars are convinced that the first husband represents the sinful disposition. The author is convinced that this interpretation of the husband is correct.[33] Thus, Paul is saying that, just as a wife is bound to her husband, so the unregenerate person is bound to his sinful disposition as master.

Interpretation of the law. Paul indicates that the law which binds the woman to her husband in the illustration represents "the law" (Romans 7:6). Here Paul uses the word "the" before the word "law," indicating that in chapter 7 he has a specific law system in mind. In light of this, scholars are convinced that by "the law" Paul means the Mosaic or old covenant law. Thus, through his illustration of marriage Paul is teaching two things. Firstly, just as a woman is bound by law to her husband, so there is some sense in which the unregenerate person under the old covenant law is bound by that law to his sinful disposition as master. Secondly, just as a woman is released from the law which bound her to her husband when death takes place, so the believer has been released from the old covenant law.

Scholars also agree that Paul includes even the moral aspect of the old covenant law in the expression "the law." That Paul does include it is evident from the fact that he quotes one of the Ten Commandments when referring to the law (Romans 7:7-8). There seems to be common agreement that Paul is teaching that believers have been released from obligation to the old covenant law, even to the moral aspect of that law.

There is disagreement, however, concerning what is involved in the believer's release from the law. Some say Paul means that the believer is freed from the penalty of the old covenant law. In other words, in Romans 7:4-6 Paul is still talking about the subject of justification. Hodge states: "Although the law continues evermore to bind us as rational creatures, it no longer prescribes the conditions of our salvation."[34]

The author disagrees with this view for several reasons. Firstly, in the earlier treatment of Romans 6 it was demonstrated that in Romans 6—8 Paul deals with the sanctification of the believer, not justification.

Secondly, as noted earlier, Romans 7 has Romans 6:14 as its antecedent and serves as an illustration of Romans 6:14. Since the issue in Romans 6:14 is sanctification and not justification, the issue in Romans 7:4-6 must also be sanctification and not justification.

Thirdly, Romans 7:5 indicates that the issue in this passage is not the penalty of the law. Paul is not talking about the effect which the law has upon those who have already violated it. Instead, he is talking about the effect of the law upon people *before* they violate it.

Fourthly, Romans 7:6 reveals that this passage deals with the issue of service, not the issue of salvation.

For these reasons the author is convinced that Paul means that the believer has been released from the entire old cove-

nant law (even its moral part) as a means of sanctification or
rule of life.

The means of release from the old covenant law. In Romans 7:1
Paul states the general principle that the law has jurisdiction
over a person as long as he lives. The implication is that only
death can break obligation to the old covenant law. In line
with this general principle Paul gives the illustration of the
wife being bound to her husband by the law of marriage until
death takes place (7:2-3). Next, Paul applies the general principle and illustration to the believer by declaring: "You also
were made to die to the Law through the body of Christ"
(verse 4); "but now we have been released from the Law,
having died to that by which we were bound" (verse 6). Paul
is teaching that the means by which the believer has been
released from the entire old covenant law as a means of
sanctification is his death with Christ. The same death which
liberated the person from all obligation to serve the sinful
disposition (Romans 6) also freed him from all obligation to
the old covenant law (Romans 7).

The purpose of release from the old covenant law. In the illustration of marriage Paul teaches that, once the wife is released
from the law of marriage, she is free to be married to another
man (Romans 7:3). In the application of the illustration he
indicates that the purpose of the believer's release from the
old covenant law is that he might be married to a new husband (7:4). While under the old covenant law as an unregenerate person, the individual had the sinful disposition as his
husband. The believer has been released from the old covenant law for the purpose of having the resurrected Christ as
his Husband.

The purpose of being married to the resurrected Christ. Paul
declares that the purpose of the believer being married to the
resurrected Christ is "that we might bear fruit for God"

(Romans 7:4). While married to the sinful disposition, the unregenerate person is caused to bear the fruit of death by that husband (7:5; 6:23). By contrast, being married to the resurrected Christ, the believer is caused to bear the fruit of God. The husband determines the offspring.

The necessity of release from the old covenant law.   In Romans 6:14 Paul implied that a person cannot be released from the position of slave to his sinful disposition until he is released from the position of being under law. Now in Romans 7:1-6 he implies that a person cannot be joined to Christ and bear fruit for God until he is released from the position of being under the old covenant law as a rule of life. Taken together these implications indicate that, in order to experience any victory over the sinful disposition and any practical sanctification, a person must be totally free from the old covenant law, even from the moral aspect of that law.

Why is it necessary for a person to be free from every aspect of the old covenant law in order to experience practical sanctification and victory over the sinful disposition? Paul answers this question in Romans 7:5, 7-25, describing the effect of the old covenant law upon the unregenerate person who is under that law. In Romans 7:14-25 he describes the effect of the old covenant law upon the believer who attempts to use it as the means for practical sanctification.

The effect of the old covenant law is the same for both the unregenerate and regenerate persons. Instead of enabling the person to live righteously, it actually hinders him from living righteously. The law does this, not because there is something evil about it; Paul is careful to declare that the old covenant law is holy, righteous, and good (Romans 7:7,12-13). Instead, the law does this because of the effect which it has upon the sinful disposition. The old covenant law has the effect of arousing the sinful disposition to assert its authority over the person more strongly than if the law never had been declared (Romans 7:5,8-13). Since the old covenant law asserts

God's authority over the person, the sinful disposition regards this assertion as a threat to what it considers its own sphere of authority. Thus, the more the law asserts itself, the more the sinful disposition exercises its power to cause the person to violate the law. Indeed, the sinful disposition actually uses the law as an opportunity for exercising its greatest strength to produce sins and death in the person. Thus, Paul says, "The sting of death is sin, and the power of sin is the law" (1 Corinthians 15:56). Paul, then, teaches an ironic fact—the old covenant law, which is holy and opposed to sin, actually serves as an instigator of more sin.

The result of release from the old covenant law.   At the end of Romans 7:6 Paul declares the result of release from the old covenant law: "We serve in newness of the Spirit and not in oldness of the letter."

Two things should be noted concerning this result. Firstly, release from the old covenant law does not result in lawlessness for the believer. Instead, it results in positive service.

Secondly, there is a qualitative difference between service in newness of the Spirit and service in oldness of the letter. The word which Paul uses for "newness" regards the new "not under aspects of *time,* but of *quality,* the new, as set over against that which has seen service, the outworn, the effete, or marred through age."[35] The word which Paul uses for "oldness" when describing service under the external, written law denotes "that which is worn out, or wearing out, by age."[36]

In light of these terms, it appears that Paul is teaching the following: through age, the external, written old covenant law has become marred and worn-out as a sphere of service. The evidence for this has been observed already. After being in effect for centuries, the old covenant law amply demonstrated the fact that, instead of enabling its subjects to live righteously, it actually hindered them through its effect upon the sinful disposition. God's answer to this problem was not to institute a new sphere of service of the same kind as the old one. He did not begin another system of external, written law which would be newer in time than the old covenant law. Instead, He employed a sphere of service which was new in the sense of being of an altogether different kind from that of the old covenant law. The new sphere was of the Spirit, not of the external, written law. It involved a new, internal disposition and a dynamic source of divine power.

This difference in quality or kind between the two spheres of service is expressed well by Bruce:

But now the Spirit supplies from within that regulative principle which once the law, and that imperfectly, supplied from without. This antithesis between "spirit" and "letter" points to the new age as that in which Jeremiah's new covenant is realized (Je. xxxi.31 ff.).[37]

Summary

Several things have been learned as a result of studying the background of the struggle of the Christian as found in Romans 6—7. When a person believes in Jesus Christ, he experiences a death with Christ. He dies in the sense that he ceases to be an "old man." He ceases to be an unregenerate man characterized by the position of slave to his sinful disposition.

Through this death the master—slave relationship which had existed between the person and his sinful disposition during the unregenerate state is terminated permanently. Never again will the sinful disposition hold the position of master over this person, and never again will this person hold the position of slave under his sinful disposition. Although the sinful disposition continues with the regenerate person through the remainder of this present life, it permanently ceases to be his master.

The reason that the sinful disposition will never be the

master of the regenerate person is the fact that the regenerate person is not under law but under grace. The same death which freed him from the former relationship with his sinful disposition also freed him from all obligation to the old covenant law. The old covenant law had actually aided the sinful disposition to maintain its position of master over the unregenerate person by arousing it to greater exercise of its authority and power. But now that the believer has been released from the authority of the law, the sinful disposition has lost this aid. Now, under grace, the regenerate person is to bear fruit for God by serving Him in the sphere of the Spirit, a qualitatively different sphere of service than that of the old covenant law. The regenerate person is not to try to bear fruit for God by using the old covenant law as his rule of life or means of sanctification.

7

THE NEW DISPOSITION AND THE STRUGGLE OF THE CHRISTIAN

The Purpose of Romans 7:14-25 in Light of Its Context

EARLIER IT WAS DEMONSTRATED that in Romans 7:14-25 Paul relates a struggle which he experienced as a Christian. A study of this passage indicates that the struggle ended in defeat. What is Paul's purpose for relating this struggle of defeat at this point in his argument? The context of the passage provides the answer.

As noted before, the antecedent of Romans 7 is Romans 6:14. There Paul declares that never again will the Christian have the sinful disposition as his master, because the Christian is not under law but under grace. In Romans 7:1-13 Paul enlarges upon this declaration in several ways. First, he demonstrates how the Christian has been released from the old covenant law. The release came by the person experiencing a death with Christ. Next, Paul shows why release from the law is absolutely necessary if a person is to bear fruit for God. The law has an ironic effect upon the unregenerate person. It arouses his sinful disposition to produce more fruit for death. Thus, the old covenant law actually hinders the unregenerate person from living righteously even though it demands perfect righteousness from him.

If Paul were to stop at verse thirteen, his argument would be incomplete. Thus far, in his attempt to show the necessity of a person being released from the law, he has demonstrated the effect of the law upon the unregenerate person only. Since the primary thing with which Paul is dealing in Romans 6:14 and Romans 7 is the concept of Christians not being under the law, Paul must deal with the effect of the law upon the regenerate person if his argument is to be complete.

On the basis of what Paul has presented thus far a person might argue that, although the old covenant law does not help the unregenerate person to live righteously, it might be far different for the regenerate person since he has the new, holy disposition within him. Perhaps all a person needs is the new disposition in order to make the old covenant law an effective means of sanctification.

In Romans 7:14-25 Paul relates what happened to him when he, as a Christian, tried to use the law as the means of practical sanctification. In spite of the fact that he had the new, holy disposition within him, the law did not enable him to live righteously. He continually experienced depressing defeat by his sinful disposition. Paul's purpose, then, for this passage is to demonstrate what he has been teaching earlier in the context—that if the Christian is to be free from the dominance of his sinful disposition, he must also be free from the old covenant law. He must never use the law as his means of practical sanctification.

Different Views Concerning the Experience which Paul Relates

Among scholars who believe that in Romans 7:14-25 Paul speaks of an experience which he had as a regenerate man there is disagreement concerning the nature and duration of the experience. Some are convinced that Paul is teaching that the Christian lives in a permanent state of helpless failure in the moral life from the time of regeneration until physical death. It is futile and wrong to rebel against this condition. The Christian should accept it as an inevitable and incurable part of the Christian experience here on earth. Victory will not come until the physical body is redeemed on the day of final redemption.[1,2]

Other scholars believe that Paul describes the experience of the regenerate person who struggles against the power or influence of his sinful disposition through his own self-effort. The self-effort is the result of using the old covenant law as the means of sanctification. Although the law tells the person what he must and must not do, it does not provide him with the power to do what is right and to abstain from what is wrong.[3] Thus, the old covenant law puts the believer in the position of having to rely upon his own power or self-effort to obey God. When that fact is joined to one seen earlier, the fact that the old covenant law actually arouses the sinful disposition to greater exercise of its power over the person in which it resides, it becomes understandable why the outcome of the struggle is defeat.

According to this view, then, throughout his Christian experience of this present life the believer is subject to the control of his sinful disposition as often as he uses the old covenant law as his means of practical sanctification. The believer is not doomed to a permanent state of defeat, however, for victory over his sinful disposition is available as often as he relies upon the grace of God as his means of sanctification. Thus, the Christian may experience either victory over or subjection to his sinful disposition interchangeably from one interval to another throughout his present life. That which determines which experience is present at any given time period is the means of sanctification relied upon by the believer during that same time period.

Evidence that Paul Describes an Attempt
to Be Sanctified by the Law

The author accepts the latter view as being the correct one. There are several evidences for concluding that Paul describes an attempt to be sanctified through self-effort as a result of relying upon the old covenant law as the means of sanctification. Firstly, the context demands this view. Since the primary thing with which Paul deals in Romans 6:14 and Romans 7 is the concept of Christians not being under the law (even the necessity of Christians not being under the law) he must deal with the effect of the law upon the regenerate person if his argument is to be complete.

Secondly, the concept of self-effort is seen very clearly in the fact that, when Paul refers to his role in the struggle, he uses the word "I" a total of twenty-four times within twelve verses (Romans 7:14-25). By contrast never once does he refer to the Holy Spirit in these verses as a participant in the struggle. However, when he relates the victory of the believer in the very next chapter (Romans 8) he refers to the Holy Spirit a total of thirteen times within the first sixteen verses.[4]

Thirdly, when Paul gives a concluding summary of the struggle (Romans 7:25), he makes the last "I" very emphatic by adding the word "myself" to it.[5] In addition, the word for "myself" is intensive and emphatic; it emphasizes identity.[6] It is obvious that Paul wants to emphasize the role of self-effort in the struggle. He does not want his readers to miss this point.

Fourthly, in Romans 7:16 Paul declares: "I agree with the Law." In verse 22 he says: "I joyfully concur with the law of God." In verse 25 he states: "I myself with my mind am serving the law of God." These expressions indicate that during his struggle Paul had the old covenant law ever before him in his thinking as a rule of life to be followed. He was attempting to keep the law for the purpose of sanctification.

Fifthly, in Romans 7:14 Paul says: "For we know that the Law is spiritual; but I am of flesh, sold into bondage to sin." Paul is drawing a contrast between the law and himself as a Christian. He could not have known of this contrast unless he had actually experienced it through an attempt to be sanctified by the law and by defeat in that attempt. The context indicates that he learned this contrast by painful experience.

The Reason Paul Could Not Be
Sanctified by the Law

Paul draws the contrast between the law and himself in Romans 7:14 in order to give the reason why he as a Christian could not be sanctified by the old covenant law: even as a Christian he is of flesh, sold into bondage to sin. The rest of the context makes it evident that this is the purpose of the contrast. The struggle and defeat which Paul describes in the remainder of the passage provide the evidence that he is of flesh and therefore cannot be sanctified by the law.

It is important to note the present tense of the verb "am" in the expression "I am of flesh, sold into bondage to sin." Paul is describing his condition in his present regenerate state. This is his condition even as he writes his Epistle to the Romans. This means, then, that the Christian is "of flesh, sold into bondage to sin."

But what could this expression possibly mean as applied to the Christian? The term translated "of flesh" means "made of flesh."[7] Paul is saying that, in spite of the fact that he is a regenerate man, he still is made of flesh.

Jesus' statement, "that which is born of the flesh is flesh" (John 3:6), seems to indicate that "flesh" refers to all that man is by human birth. As flesh man is weak (Matthew 26:41; Romans 6:19).

Robinson says that "flesh represents mere man, man in contrast with God—hence man in his weakness and mortality."[8] A strong point of contrast, then, between man as creature and God as creator lies in the sphere of power: "Contrasted with God, who is essentially Spirit, Power . . . man is impotent. 'Infirmity' is an inherent quality. . ." of man as flesh.[9] Thus, when Paul says that he is made of flesh, he is emphasizing the fact that, even though he is a regenerate man with a new disposition, two things are true of him: (1) he is still only a man, and (2) apart from divine empowerment he is powerless to do the will of God.

Paul further defines what it means to be "of flesh" by indicating that it also involves "having been sold under sin" (7:14, literal translation). Since, as noted earlier, Paul in Romans 6 and 7 uses the term "sin" to refer to the sinful disposition, the expression "having been sold under sin" implies bondage to the sinful disposition. He is saying that there is some sense in which he as a Christian is still in bondage to the sinful disposition.

Prior to the fall of man human flesh was not subject to a sinful disposition. In fact, prior to the fall it did not possess a sinful disposition. But when the first man, Adam, chose to disobey God, he thereby sold human flesh into bondage under the sinful disposition. As a result, human flesh acquired a new characteristic: bondage under the sinful disposition. With the exception of Jesus Christ, who became human flesh (John 1:14) without a sinful disposition, every human being born since the fall has been born in that bondage.

This bondage involves three things: the presence of the sinful disposition in human flesh, the sinful disposition holding the position of master over human flesh, and human flesh being subject to the power of the sinful disposition. The unregenerate person is subject to all three aspects of this bondage.

Earlier it was seen that the sinful disposition loses its position of master over a person when that person becomes regenerate. In that sense the regenerate person has been freed from bondage to sin (Romans 6:7). But the sinful disposition continues present in the regenerate person throughout this present life, and the regenerate person is susceptible to the power of the sinful disposition whenever he relies upon his own self-effort rather than the power of the Holy Spirit for enablement to live a godly life.

The regenerate person, then, as a result of being made of flesh, is still in bondage in the sense that the sinful disposition continues present in him and in the sense that he is susceptible to that disposition's power. It is in these senses that Paul, as a regenerate man, could say that he is of flesh, having been sold under sin.

The Result of the Attempt to Be Sanctified by the Law

The result of Paul's attempt to be sanctified by the law was a confusing struggle which he could not understand (Romans 7:15). On the one hand he knew that the law was good (verse 16); he joyfully concurred with it (verse 22); he served the law with his mind (verse 25); he wished to do good (verses 18-19,21); he hated evil (verses 15,19). But on the other hand he ended up doing the evil which he hated and not doing the good which he wished to do (verses 15,19). This great contrast between desire and performance caused real confusion. Paul could not understand why he couldn't live right since the law was good and since he agreed with it and desired to keep it.

The Activity of the New Disposition

Earlier it was demonstrated that Paul as a regenerate man possessed the new disposition. The fact that he did possess the new disposition gives rise to an interesting question. What did the new disposition do for Paul in his struggle with his sinful disposition?

Since Paul was attempting to be sanctified by the old covenant law, and since the new disposition consists of the law of God written in the heart, it would seem natural to expect that the new disposition would cause Paul to be favorably oriented toward the old covenant law. Paul gives several indications that he had such an orientation. Firstly, in Romans 7:16 he declares: "I agree with the Law, confessing that it is good." Secondly, in verse 25 he states: "I myself with my mind am serving the law of God." Since the mind is internal, it would appear that something inside of Paul was prompting this service. The author is convinced that that internal something was the new disposition, since it is the law internalized.

Thirdly, in Romans 7:22 Paul says: "For I joyfully concur with the law of God in the inner man." The word translated "I joyfully concur" is much stronger in meaning than the word translated "I agree with" in verse 16;[10] it carries the idea of rejoicing with someone or something.[11] "It is the agreement of moral sympathy."[12]

Paul indicates that this joyful concurrence took place in the inner man. Thus, "this delight is not peripheral but belongs to that which is deepest and inmost in his moral and spiritual being."[13] Paul is saying that the new disposition inside him caused his inner self to have this strong, favorable orientation toward the old covenant law. Nothing could be more radically opposed to the inward orientation of enmity which the sinful disposition causes the unregenerate person to have against God and the old covenant law (Romans 8:7).

The new disposition also had an interesting effect upon Paul's will. It is important to note that the new disposition and the will of a person are not the same thing. A person has a will throughout life, but he does not have the new disposition until he is regenerated.

During Paul's struggle the new disposition worked upon his will to prompt him to will to do what the old covenant law said was right and not to do what the law said was wrong. Paul indicates this in Romans 7:18-19 where he says: "For the wishing is present in me, but the doing of the good is not. For the good that I wish, I do not do; but I practice the very evil that I do not wish."

The word that is translated "wish" "here denotes definite purpose and readiness to do the divine will. . . . Thus the [wishing] of R[omans] 7 is the inner intention of man to keep the Law which, grounded though it is in pleasure in the Law, never goes beyond the stage of intention."[14] Thus, "we see in R[omans] 7 the impotence of legal man according to Paul. This man wills and fails to do, and does what he does not will (vs. 18, cf. 16,19)."[15]

It would appear, then, that the new disposition did several things for Paul in his struggle. It caused him to agree with the law of God, to serve the law with his mind, and to have moral sympathy with the law in his inner self. In addition, it prompted him to will to do what the law said was good and not to do what the law said was evil.

This activity of the new disposition inside Paul gives insight concerning the function of the new disposition inside the regenerate person, whether or not that person is attempting to be sanctified by the old covenant law. Since the old covenant law was an expression of the holy nature and will of God, one can conclude that the new disposition does the following for the regenerate person: it causes him to agree with, to serve with his mind, and to have moral sympathy with the holy nature and will of God in his inner self. In other words, it causes him to be favorably oriented toward God. In addition, the new disposition prompts the regenerate person to will to do the will of God.

Gutzke expresses the activity of the new disposition as follows:

When I am born again, it is to the praise of God and to the joy of the Christian that I will find within me promptings to want to do what is pleasing to Him "who loved me, and gave himself for me" (Gal. 2:20). . . . In this new nature . . . I want to do God's will and share in God's work, helping to spread the Gospel and seeing other people saved. . . . When I become a Christian, I find that this new nature is beginning to influence my ideas and to affect my actions."[16]

The Presence of the Sinful Disposition

If the regenerate person had only the new disposition inside him, he probably would have no problem doing the will of God. But, as seen earlier, he also has the sinful disposition inside him. The believer is still subject to its presence and influence.

Paul gives several indications that the sinful disposition is still present in him. Firstly, in Romans 7:14 he says: "I am of flesh, sold under sin" (literal translation). As noted before, Paul is saying that the sinful disposition is still with him, and it dominates him as often as it can.

Secondly, Paul talks about "sin which indwells me" (Romans 7:17); "sin which dwells in me" (verse 20); "evil is present in me" (verse 21); and "the law of sin which is in my members" (verse 23).

Thirdly, in Romans 6:12-13 Paul gives the following commands to Christians:

Therefore do not let sin reign in your mortal body that you should obey its lusts, and do not go on presenting the members of your body to sin as instruments of unrighteousness; but present yourselves to God as those alive from the dead, and your members as instruments of righteousness to God.

If the sinful disposition were no longer resident in Christians as a powerful force, these commands would not be necessary.[17]

Fourthly, if the sinful disposition were not in the Christian, then the struggle between the Holy Spirit and the flesh of the Christian described in Galatians 5:17 would not take place.[18]

Fifthly, Paul indicates that God gave him his thorn in the flesh to prevent him from exalting himself (2 Corinthians 12:7). If Paul had not had the sinful disposition within him even as an apostle, there would have been no danger of his exalting himself.[19]

In light of the continuing presence of the sinful disposition inside the regenerate person, the following can be said of Paul:

He was sold under sin as a child of the first Adam, and he delighted in the law of God as a child of the second Adam. Accordingly, through the whole of the passage to the end of the chapter, Paul . . . points to two distinct natures operating within him.[20]

The Activity of the Sinful Disposition

As a result of the believer's death with Christ, the sinful disposition has lost its legal position of master over him. In spite of this loss of position, the sinful disposition attempts illegally to exercise power over the Christian.

Paul makes it clear that not only is the sinful disposition inside him as a regenerate person, but also it is an extremely active force. It exercises great power to make him go contrary to what his inner self wills. Paul portrays the activity of his sinful disposition in two ways. Firstly, in Romans 7:17,20 he pictures the sinful disposition as an unwanted guest that not only lives in another person's house but also takes control of that house against the owner's wishes.[21] In essence Paul is saying: "Now that I am regenerate I hate the fact that the sinful disposition is still in me. It is continually usurping control of me against my will."

Secondly, in Romans 7:23 Paul portrays the sinful disposition as an armed soldier that wages war against the law of his mind and makes him a prisoner of itself. Since law is intended to function as a controlling factor, it would appear that by "the law of my mind" Paul is referring to his mind as a controlling factor. "The law of sin" is a reference to the sinful disposition as a controlling factor. Thus, Paul is teaching that, when his mind sought to control him to serve the old covenant law (verse 25), the sinful disposition waged war against that control and triumphed by taking Paul captive in its own control.

These portrayals of the activity of the sinful disposition give insight concerning the function of the sinful disposition within the regenerate person. The sinful disposition wages war against that which would control the believer for good or for service to God. It works to cause the believer to go contrary to what his inner self wills in accord with the holy nature and will of God. It strives to take the regenerate person captive in its own control. In other words, although it has lost its legal position of master over the believer, it tries illegally to exercise controlling power over him.

The Outcome of the Struggle

The outcome of Paul's struggle which he describes in Romans 7:14-25 can be stated in one word: defeat. Paul says that he ended up doing the evil which he hated, and he failed to do the good which he willed to do (verses 15-16,19-20). He was in the exasperating situation of being held a prisoner contrary to his will (verse 23). In all his efforts to do right and to abstain from evil he was blocked by a power which he could not overcome (verses 22-23). In great frustration he gave vocal expression to the wretchedness which he felt (verse 24). In spite of his being a regenerate man with the new disposition, all his efforts ended in utter, degrading defeat.

The Reason for Defeat

Paul recognizes the reason for his defeat when he says: "For the wishing is present in me, but the doing of the good is not" (Romans 7:18). The old covenant law, which he was relying upon as his means of sanctification, did not give him the power to overcome the power of the sinful disposition and to do the good. Instead, it actually aroused the sinful disposition to a greater exercise of its power against Paul (verses 7-13). Since the law did not provide him with the power of performance, Paul was forced to resort to self-effort in his struggle with the sinful disposition. But that didn't work either, for even his regenerated humanity by itself lacked the power of performance. The new disposition within his inner self did positive things for him, but it did not give him the power to overcome the power of the sinful disposition and to do the good. Whenever Paul resorted to self-effort to do good, the sinful disposition rendered him helpless. The reason for his defeat was lack of power.

Kelly comments:

Guilt is not the matter in hand, but power, or rather the total absence of it; so that, with the best possible dispositions and desires, all ends in captivity to sin, though it is now hated. It is not the soul in the death and darkness of nature, but renewed. God is loved, evil abhorred; but the soul finds itself powerless either to give effect to the one or to avoid the other.[22]

Paul's defeat gives insight concerning three matters. Firstly, the old covenant law is powerless as a means of sanctification even for the believer. Secondly, although the new disposition does positive things for the believer, it has a limitation. It does not give the power necessary to do the good. Thirdly, if the Christian is to do what God says is right, two things must be true of him: he must will to do it, and he must have the power to do it. Living a righteous life is more than a matter of the will. To have will without power leaves the believer frustrated and unable to accomplish his purposes.

The Cry for Help

In Romans 7:24 Paul calls himself a "wretched man." The term which he uses indicates a wretchedness which comes through the exhaustion of hard labor.[23] Paul had struggled so long and strenuously through self-effort against the sinful disposition that he had exhausted all his strength. With no reserve left upon which to draw he collapses in the clutches of the sinful disposition.

While in this desperate plight, Paul finally recognizes that he himself does not possess the power necessary to overcome the controlling power of the sinful disposition and to do the good. It dawns upon him that if he is ever to get victory over sin someone else must provide that victory for him. Thus, in desperation, he cries for help: "Who will set me free from the body of this death?"

The term "set free" denotes "the act of a soldier who runs at his comrade's cry to rescue him from the hands of the enemy."[24] In essence Paul was saying, "Isn't there someone who can intervene on my behalf to rescue me from the controlling power of the sinful disposition?"

In light of Paul's experience of defeat, an important question could be asked at this point. Does Paul's experience indicate that the believer is condemned to live in continual defeat under the controlling power of the sinful disposition?

The Provision of Victory

Immediately after uttering his plea for help, Paul, in Romans 7:25, interjects a strong, sudden expression of gratitude: "Thanks be to God through Jesus Christ our Lord!"

Concerning this expression Hodge writes: "The great blessing of deliverance for which he gives thanks, is received through the Lord Jesus Christ. He does for us what neither the law nor our own powers could effect."[25]

By the time Paul wrote Romans he had learned that the Christian is not condemned to live in defeat always. Having learned that God has provided a means for victory through Christ, he interjects this expression of gratitude as a ray of hope in the midst of this account of despair. In Romans 8 he presents what God has done through Christ for victory. This will be examined later, but for now it is sufficient to note that the Christian does not have to be defeated always. Whenever he appropriates what God has provided, he can experience victory.

Conclusions

The study of Paul's struggle as recorded in Romans 7:14-25 has led to several conclusions. Firstly, Paul describes the experience of the regenerate person who struggles against the power of the sinful disposition through his own self-effort.

Secondly, the new disposition causes the believer to agree with, to serve, and joyfully to concur with the holy nature and will of God in the inner self. It also prompts him to will to do what God says is right and to avoid what God says is wrong.

Thirdly, the sinful disposition is still present and active in the believer. It wages war against him. Through its controlling power it defeats the believer every time he struggles against it through his own self-effort. It forces the believer to go contrary to what he wills in accord with the holy nature and will of God.

Fourthly, the new disposition is limited in what it can do. It does not provide the believer with the power necessary to overpower the sinful disposition and to do what God says is right. The regenerate person needs more than the new disposition; he also needs a great source of power.

Fifthly, the regenerate person is not condemned to live in a permanent state of defeat. God has provided a means for victory over the power of the sinful disposition through Jesus Christ.

8

THE NEW DISPOSITION AND
THE HOLY SPIRIT

The Agent of the New Disposition

THE HOLY SPIRIT is related to the new disposition of the Christian in at least two ways. In the first place, the Holy Spirit is the agent by whom Jesus Christ implanted the new disposition in the Christian. In 2 Corinthians 3:3 Paul says to Christians: "You are a letter of Christ . . . written not with ink, but with the Spirit of the living God, not on tablets of stone, but on tablets of human hearts." As noted earlier, that which was written on the heart was the law of God or the new disposition. Paul is saying that Jesus Christ uses the Holy Spirit to place the new disposition in the believer through regeneration.

The Powerful Ally of the New Disposition

The second way in which the Holy Spirit is related to the new disposition is that the Holy Spirit works together with the new disposition to enable the Christian to do God's will. The new disposition prompts the believer to will to do what is right. The Holy Spirit supplies the power necessary to put that will into effect. Both the Old and New Testaments indicate that this is the function of the Holy Spirit.

Ezekiel 36:26-27

As noted earlier in Ezekiel's prophecy concerning the new covenant, God promised not only to put a new human spirit (the new disposition) within the regenerate person but also to put His Spirit within him. As a result of this, the regenerate person would submit to God's rule.

In this passage, God's concept is that of the Holy Spirit being in the regenerate person for the purpose of empowering him to do what God wants. Snaith declares that in the Old Testament "the idea of a more-than-human power runs through the whole of the use of the phrase [Spirit of the Lord]. As a result of this special endowment of divine power men are able to do that which, in the ordinary way and relying upon purely human resources, they are quite unable to do."[1] Again he says that the phrase "Spirit of the Lord" "stands for that special power by which God inspires the individual man, enabling him to do the will of God, and thus to do those things which in his own strength he is wholly unable to do."[2]

Romans 8:1-4

Concerning the function of the Holy Spirit in the New Testament, Snaith states that in Paul's writings the Spirit of God "takes hold of a man, controls him, gives to him a power that is not his own. . . . He is God Himself, manifest once in the flesh in the Lord Jesus Christ, and now manifest in human lives."[3] He is "a transforming Power."[4] That Snaith is correct can be seen from several New Testament passages.

Immediately after talking about the defeat of the Christian and God's provision of victory through Jesus Christ, Paul enlarges upon the provision by writing Romans 8:1-4.

The Announcement of No Condemnation

In Romans 8:1 Paul makes the following announcement:

"There is therefore now no condemnation for those who are in Christ Jesus." Scholars disagree concerning what Paul means by "no condemnation." Some believe that Paul is referring to the believer's justification from the guilt of sin.[5]

Others believe that Paul is saying that the believer is not condemned to a life of servitude to the sinful disposition. Bruce is convinced that the term "condemnation" refers to "penal servitude" and that Paul is teaching that "there is no reason why those who are 'in Christ Jesus' should go on doing penal servitude as though they had never been pardoned and never been liberated from the prison-house of sin."[6]

The author agrees with the latter view for several reasons. Firstly, Romans 6—8 deals with the subject of sanctification, not justification. As a result the first view would be contrary to the context.

Secondly, the next verse (Romans 8:2), which presents the reason why believers are under no condemnation, deals with freedom from the controlling power of the sinful disposition, not with freedom from guilt. This will be demonstrated later.

Thirdly, the sentence in which the words "no condemnation" appear is joined to the immediately preceding context by the word "therefore." This indicates that Romans 8:1 is a conclusion drawn from what Paul has just said in Romans 7. Since Paul has just dealt with the problem of the believer being overpowered by the sinful disposition and God's provision of deliverance from the power of that disposition (7:24-25), his conclusion in Romans 8:1 must be referring to no condemnation with regard to the power of the sinful disposition, not to no condemnation with regard to guilt. Paul is saying that, since God has provided the believer with deliverance from the power of the sinful disposition, the believer is not condemned to a life of servitude to that disposition.

Paul's use of the word "now" in his announcement of no condemnation indicates that the believer is free from this condemnation *now*, during this present lifetime. He does not have to wait until death or future glorification to have freedom from servitude to the sinful disposition.

The Reason for No Condemnation

Paul begins Romans 8:2 with the word "for." This indicates that he is giving the reason for the believer not being condemned to a life of servitude to the sinful disposition: "The law of the Spirit of life in Christ Jesus has set you free from the law of sin and of death." In other words, God has provided a means of deliverance. That means is the law of the Spirit of life.

Several significant things should be noted concerning Paul's statement in Romans 8:2. Firstly, he refers to two distinct laws: the law of the Spirit of life and the law of sin and death. Law, no matter what kind it may be, is established for the purpose of governing or controlling. In light of this, the law of the Spirit of life is the controlling power of the Holy Spirit, which controlling power produces newness of life (Romans 6:4; 7:6).[7] As noted earlier (7:23), the law of sin is the controlling power of the sinful disposition, which controlling power works death.[8] The reason that the believer is not condemned to a life of servitude to the sinful disposition is that the controlling power of the Holy Spirit has set him free from the controlling power of the sinful disposition.

Secondly, the freedom from the sinful disposition to which Paul refers in Romans 8:2 is different from the freedom from that same disposition to which he refers in Romans 6:7. Two things indicate this. Firstly, Paul uses two distinct words for freedom in these passages. As noted earlier, the word in 6:7 is a legal term. The word in 8:2 is not a legal term. Secondly, the freedoms of these two passages are obtained through two different means. The freedom of 6:7 is obtained through death with Christ; the freedom of 8:2 is obtained through the controlling power of the Holy Spirit.

The sense in which the two freedoms differ is that the

freedom of Romans 6:7 involves freedom from a position; the freedom of Romans 8:2 involves freedom from a controlling power. As seen earlier, in Romans 6:1-14 Paul teaches that through death with Christ the person's position of slave and his sinful disposition's position of master are terminated once-for-all. Never again will the sinful disposition hold the position of master over that person.

Although the sinful disposition has lost its position of master over the believer, it still remains with him and tries to exercise control over him. Even if the believer reckons that he no longer holds the position of slave under his sinful disposition, he cannot experience freedom from its controlling power as long as he tries to gain that freedom through self-effort. Every time the believer tries to get away from the controlling power of his former master on his own, it takes him captive against his will. Unless someone more powerful than the sinful disposition intervenes on behalf of the believer and sets him free from the controlling power of his former master, the believer is doomed to a life of servitude to a disposition which has no right to exercise power over him.

In Romans 8:2 Paul is saying that someone more powerful than the sinful disposition *has* intervened on behalf of the believer and *has* set him free from the controlling power of his former master. That someone is the Holy Spirit.

The tense of the verb translated "has set free" indicates that the Holy Spirit set the believer free in the past. Shedd is convinced that this refers "to the time and act of regeneration, when the freedom was begun and established."[9] In the past, when the believer was regenerated, the Holy Spirit established freedom from the controlling power of the sinful disposition.

The author is convinced that Shedd is correct. At the time of regeneration the believer is indwelt by the Holy Spirit. This is evident from the fact that "if anyone does not have the Spirit of Christ, he does not belong to Him" (Romans 8:9). Certainly it is the indwelling of the Holy Spirit which provides the basis for the Spirit's controlling power being made available to the believer.

Although the Holy Spirit set the believer free at the time of regeneration, the believer does not always experience that freedom. When he uses self-effort against the power of the sinful disposition (such as when he relies upon the old covenant law as the means of sanctification), he experiences domination by sin. Only when he appropriates the controlling power of the Holy Spirit, as a result of relying upon God's grace as the means of sanctification, does he experience the freedom that is his.

Paul teaches that the "no condemnation" (Romans 8:1) is to those who are "in Christ Jesus" and that the law of the Spirit of life is "in Christ Jesus" (verse 2). The implication is that these things are true as a result of the believer's union with Christ. This concept of union with Christ reverts back to Paul's teaching in Romans 6:3-5 and 7:4. There Paul teaches that believers have been united with Christ in the likeness of His death and in the likeness of His resurrection.

Through union with Christ in the likeness of His death the believer has been freed from the position of slave under the sinful disposition. Through union with Christ in the likeness of His resurrection the believer has been freed from the controlling power of the sinful disposition. The latter freedom makes it possible for the believer to "walk in newness of life" (Romans 6:4), to "serve in newness of the Spirit and not in oldness of the letter" (7:6) and to "bear fruit for God" (7:4). He has been set free to do what his inner self wills to do: the will of God.

The Reason for Freedom

From what has been seen it is evident that the grace of God through the power of the Holy Spirit is able to do something which the old covenant law through the self-effort of the believer is not able to do: free the believer from the controlling power of his sinful disposition.

In Romans 8:3 Paul gives the reason why the grace of God can do what the old covenant law could not. It is because God did something which the old covenant law was power-less to do: condemn sin in the flesh.

In what sense did God condemn the sinful disposition in the flesh? There are two possibilities: firstly, He con-demned it in the sense of pronouncing a sentence of judg-ment upon it; or secondly, He condemned it in the sense of actually executing judgment upon it.[10]

For several reasons the author is convinced that Paul is primarily using the second sense in Romans 8:3. Firstly, the condemning of sin which God did is something which the old covenant law could not do. Certainly the old covenant law pronounced a sentence of judgment upon sin, but it could not execute judgment upon it in the sense of nullifying its power within a human being. Indeed, the old covenant law actually aroused the sinful disposition to a more vigorous exercise of its power.

Secondly, the verb which Paul uses for "condemned" carries the idea of execution of judgment as well as pro-nouncement of judgment when used of divine condemnation as it is here.[11]

The reason why the old covenant law could not execute judgment upon the sinful disposition in the sense of nullifying its power within a human being was that it was weak through the flesh. The old covenant law was totally external to human beings. It could pronounce sentences of judgment against the sinful disposition from outside the person, but it could not get into human flesh to execute judgment upon the sinful disposi-tion in the very sphere of its activity.

The inability of the old covenant law to execute judg-ment within human flesh forced the law to rely upon human flesh itself to execute judgment against the sinful disposition. But, as noted earlier, one of the major ideas associated with human flesh is that of weakness. Human flesh by itself does not possess the power necessary to execute judgment upon the sinful disposition. Thus, the law was rendered weak through the very instrument upon which it relied for strength.

The manner in which God executed judgment upon the sinful disposition in human flesh was this: He sent "His own Son in the likeness of sinful flesh and for sin." Through the incarnation God placed His Son in the sphere of human flesh, the very sphere in which the sinful disposition operates. The incarnated Son of God was a powerful enemy of the sinful disposition who could execute judgment upon it within its own sphere.

It is important to note that, although Christ became flesh (John 1:14), His flesh was void of the sinful disposition. Thus, Paul does not say that God sent His Son in sinful flesh, but in the likeness of sinful flesh.

If Christ's flesh was void of the sinful disposition, then how did Christ execute judgment upon that disposition in the flesh? This is difficult to answer. Some scholars say that it was through the death of Christ that God executed judgment upon the sinful disposition in the sense of nullifying its power in human flesh.[12] They support their view with 1 Peter 2:24, which indicates that Christ died in order that believers might live to righteousness. Since, as is being seen in Romans 8, believers are able to live righteously only as a result of God executing judgment upon sin, the death of Christ must have great bearing upon the execution of this judgment.

Others say that God executed judgment upon sin through the holy life which Christ lived.[13] Throughout His life Christ did God's will perfectly, obeying even unto death (Philippians 2:7-8). Thus, Christ executed judgment upon the sinful disposition by totally excluding it and its power from His human flesh throughout a whole lifetime. For the first time since the fall of man the sinful disposition had not been able to inhabit or exercise controlling power over human flesh. Its power had been nullified in human flesh by a greater power. Now, that greater power is available to those who are united with Christ.

Since both views seem to have scriptural support, the author is led to believe that God executed judgment upon the sinful disposition through both the life and death of Christ.

The Purpose of the Condemnation of Sin

In Romans 8:4 Paul states that the purpose for which God condemned sin in the flesh is "that the requirement of the Law might be fulfilled in us." Paul is saying that God executed judgment upon the sinful disposition for the purpose that the holy life required by the old covenant law might be fulfilled in the believer.

It is important to note that the passive voice of the verb translated "might be fulfilled" indicates that the believer does not produce this holy life in himself. The Holy Spirit produces it in and for him through His power. Thus, the Holy Spirit produces what the old covenant law demanded but could not produce.

The Appropriation of the Means of Freedom

Earlier it was noted that, although the Holy Spirit set the believer free from the controlling power of the sinful disposition at the time of regeneration, the believer does not always experience that freedom. The reason for his not experiencing that freedom is this: he does not always appropriate the controlling power of the Holy Spirit, the means of freedom from the controlling power of the sinful disposition.

Because this is so, at the end of Romans 8:4 Paul declares that the holy life required by the old covenant law will be fulfilled in those "who do not walk according to the flesh, but according to the Spirit." Paul's point is twofold. Firstly, those believers who walk according to the power of the flesh (the power of their own humanity) will not have the holy life required by the law fulfilled in them. The power of the flesh is no match for the power of the sinful disposition; thus, they will be controlled by the power of that disposition. This was Paul's problem in Romans 7:14-25.

Secondly, those believers who walk according to the power of the Holy Spirit will have the holy life required by the law fulfilled in them. The power of the Spirit will over-come the power of the sinful disposition and enable the believer to do God's will.

Paul uses the concept of walking for a purpose. The appropriation of the power of the Spirit is not a once-for-all act which delivers the believer from the controlling power of his sinful disposition forever. Just as walking is a step-by-step procedure, so the appropriation of the controlling power of the Holy Spirit is a moment-by-moment procedure. During those moments when the believer is depending upon the power of his own humanity to enable him to have victory over sin, his sinful disposition will take control of him against his will. During those moments when he is depending upon the power of the Holy Spirit, he will experience freedom from the sinful disposition's control, and his life will be character-ized by holiness.

Ephesians 3:16-19

In Ephesians 3:16-19 Paul prays for Christians that God:

Would grant you, according to the riches of His glory, to be strength-ened with power through His Spirit in the inner man; so that Christ may dwell in your hearts through faith; and that you, being rooted and grounded in love, may be able to comprehend with all the saints what is the breadth and length and height and depth, and to know the love of Christ which surpasses knowledge, that you may be filled up to all the fullness of God.

In Ephesians 3:16 Paul prays that his readers would be strengthened with divine power through the agency of the Holy Spirit. The fact that Paul prays for this to happen indi-cates that, although the potential for strengthening is there, the actual strengthening itself may not have taken place as yet. When this concept is joined to the fact that the power of the Holy Spirit was made available to the believer at the time of regeneration (Romans 8:2), it becomes apparent that the actual strengthening depends upon the appropriation of the power of the Spirit by the believer. Concerning this, Kent writes: "The Spirit comes to reside in each believer at regeneration, but must be relied upon continually to furnish power for Christian living."[14]

Paul requests that the strengthening take place in "the inner man," the very place where, as noted earlier, the new disposition (the law of God in the heart) resides and functions and where Paul as a regenerate man joyfully concurred in the law of God (Romans 7:22). Paul's prayer is consistent with what was seen in Romans 7:14-25. Since the new disposition in the inner man prompts the believer to will God's will but does not give him the power necessary to do God's will, the believer needs to be strengthened with power through the Spirit in his inner man in order to do God's will.

In verse 17 Paul presents the intended purpose of the strengthening with power through the Spirit: "So that Christ may dwell in your hearts." Paul cannot be praying that Christ may dwell in their hearts as Saviour, for he is making this request for Christians. They already had Christ dwelling in their hearts as Saviour.

It would appear that Paul has in mind the holy life of Christ dwelling in believers. The power of the Spirit can make the believer more and more like Jesus Christ in daily living. Kent expresses it this way:

Inasmuch as these words clearly refer to the Ephesian Christians, Paul cannot be referring to the initial indwelling of believers by Christ in the person of the Holy Spirit. Rather, he is speaking of the further and richer dwelling which occurs as Christ takes possession of more and more of us. This is expressed elsewhere as "filling."[15]

Thus, the dwelling of Christ in the believer which Paul has in mind is a progressive thing.

It is important to note the means by which this dwelling

of Christ takes place: "through faith." As the believer trusts the Holy Spirit rather than his own humanity to make him more like Christ, the Spirit empowers him to experience the progressive fulfillment of that goal.

According to Ephesians 3:19 Paul wants Christians to "be filled up to all the fulness of God."

"God's fullness is that with which He is filled, and denotes the perfections and excellencies He possesses."[16] Since man can never possess such excellencies of deity as omnipotence, omniscience, and omnipresence, this must be a reference to God's moral excellencies. Paul is saying that he wants Christians to be filled with the fullness of God's moral character.

This being filled with the fullness of God's moral character is also a progressive thing, to be completed only after the believer has gone to be with Christ. The evidence for this is presented by Bruce who points out that the preposition which is translated "to"

> ... suggests rather their being progressively filled "up to the measure of" God's fulness ... in Christ the divine fulness is ideally theirs already, but his earnest desire is that it may increasingly be realized in their experience. In Colossians 2:19 he dwells upon the process, increasing "with the increase of God"; here he dwells upon the consummation.[17]

Thus, being filled unto the fullness of God's moral character, becoming fully Christlike, and having the righteousness demanded by the old covenant law fulfilled in the believer are all progressive things. It appears that they all refer to the same thing: progressive sanctification. In addition, they all are produced through the same means: the power of the Holy Spirit. They develop step-by-step inside the Christian throughout his lifetime as the Holy Spirit gives him one victory after another over the controlling power of the sinful disposition. Thus, many skirmishes can be won during the course of the believer's life as he appropriates the power of the Holy Spirit, but the whole war is not completed in victory until the believer has gone to be with Christ.

Conclusions

As a result of what has been seen, two things can be said concerning the relationship of the Holy Spirit to the new disposition: the Holy Spirit is the agent who writes the law of God in the heart of the believer at the time of regeneration, thereby giving the believer the new disposition which prompts the believer to will to do God's will; and the Holy Spirit is the ally who frees the believer from the controlling power of the sinful disposition at the time of regeneration, thereby making available the power necessary for the believer to put his will into effect. The Holy Spirit enables the new disposition to do more than affect the will. He enables it to govern the whole person, even the person's body.

An excellent summary of this twofold relationship between the new disposition and the Holy Spirit is found in Philippians 2:13: "God is the one who works in you both to will and to work on behalf of His good will" (literal translation). Paul is saying that God works two things in the Christian: the willing of His will, and the doing of His will. He works the willing by giving the believer the new disposition through the regenerating work of the Holy Spirit. He works the doing by giving the believer the controlling power of the indwelling Holy Spirit.

The Master—Slave Analogy

Earlier it was noted that Paul uses the master—slave analogy as a vehicle to help him make the spiritual truths of Romans 6—8 understandable. Now that the teaching of Romans 6—8 has been examined, the author will use that same kind of analogy in order to summarize Paul's teaching in those chapters.

Prior to the middle of the 1800s slavery was a legal institution in America. It was supported by the law of the land. Slaveholders held the legal position of master over human beings, and those human beings held the position of slave. Because the slaveholders held the legal position of master, the law gave them the right to dominate and control every aspect of their slaves' beings and lives, and the slaves had no choice but to render complete obedience to the dictates of their masters.

By analogy Paul says (Romans 6:16-20) that it is the same kind of relationship which exists between the unregenerate person and his sinful disposition. The sinful disposition holds the legal position of master over the unregenerate person, and the unregenerate person holds the position of slave under his sinful disposition. Because the sinful disposition holds the legal position of master, it has the right to dominate and control every aspect of the unregenerate person's total being and life, and the unregenerate person has no choice but to render complete obedience to the dictates of his sinful disposition.

When the government of the United States abolished slavery as a legal institution in the middle of the 1800s, immediately slaveholders lost their legal position of master, and the slaves lost the position of slave. No longer did the former masters have the right to dominate or control the former slaves, and no longer were the former slaves obligated to continue serving their former masters. The former slaves were freed legally from their former masters. Now they had a choice. They could choose to continue serving their former masters if they so desired, or they could choose to leave the plantation and no longer serve.

By analogy Paul teaches (Romans 6:1-10) that the same change of relationship takes place between the unregenerate person and his sin nature when that person experiences death with Christ. When the unregenerate person trusts Christ as Saviour, he dies with Christ in the sense that he ceases to be an unregenerate person. Immediately the sinful disposition loses its position of master over him, and he loses his position of slave. No longer does the sinful disposition have the right to dominate or control its former slave, and no longer is the person obligated to continue serving the sinful disposition. The person has been freed legally from the sinful disposition. It remains with him and will continue to attempt to exercise controlling power over him (now illegally), but it has lost forever its position of master over him. Now, as a believer, the person has a choice. He may choose to continue serving his sinful disposition if he so desires, or he may choose to stop serving.

Although it was a fact that the United States government had abolished slavery and had thereby ended master—slave relationships, that fact did the former slaves no practical good unless they took it into account in their thinking. Only when they reckoned on the fact of their change of position—that they had lost their position of slave and no longer had a master—did they try to leave the plantations and enjoy the freedom which had been granted to them.

By analogy Paul indicates (Romans 6:11) that, although it is a fact that the master—slave relationship between the unregenerate person and his sin nature ends when that person dies with Christ, that fact does that person no practical good unless he takes it into account in his thinking. Only when the believer reckons on the fact of his change of position—that he has lost his position of slave and that his sinful disposition has lost its position of master—will he try to enjoy the freedom from required service to his sinful disposition which has been granted to him.

Even when former slaves in the United States reckoned on the fact of their change of position and thereby left the plantations to enjoy their freedom, sometimes their former masters tracked them down, captured them, and dragged them back to the plantations against their wills to force further service out of them. For some this happened repeatedly each time they attempted to get away on their own initiative. They had been set free from their position of slave, but now their problem was that of obtaining freedom from the controlling power which their former masters exercised over them illegally.

By analogy Paul teaches (Romans 7:14-25) that a similar thing can happen to the believer. Even when he reckons on the fact that he has lost his position of slave and thereby chooses to stop serving his sinful disposition, it will capture him against his will and force further service out of him. This will happen repeatedly each time the believer tries in his own strength to do what God says is right. He has been set free from his position of slave, but now his problem is that of obtaining freedom from the controlling power which his sinful disposition exercises over him illegally.

In order to obtain freedom from the controlling power of their former masters, the former slaves needed a greater power to intervene on their behalf and overpower their former masters. The United States government provided that greater power for them in the form of a division of the army. In order to experience the freedom which this greater power provided, the former slaves had to trust the army rather than themselves to overpower their former masters.

By analogy Paul points out (Romans 8:1-4) that the same is true for the believer. In order to obtain freedom from the controlling power of his sinful disposition, the believer needs a greater power to intervene on his behalf and overpower the sinful disposition. God has provided that greater power for the believer through the indwelling Holy Spirit. In order to experience the freedom which God has provided, the believer must trust the Holy Spirit rather than himself to overpower the sinful disposition.

9

THE NEW DISPOSITION, THE NEW MAN, AND THE IMAGE OF GOD AND CHRIST

The New Disposition and the New Man

Definition of the New Man

THOSE WHO BELIEVE that the expression "old man" refers to the sinful disposition are convinced that the expression "new man" refers to the new disposition.[1] Consistency demands that they equate the new disposition with the new man.

That the old man is not the sinful disposition was demonstrated earlier when Romans 6 was examined. At that time it was noted that the old man is the unregenerate man or the human person in his unregenerate state. As an old man, the unsaved person holds the position of slave under the sinful disposition and is characterized by the sinful way of life. Through death with Christ the person stops being an old man, for he dies in the sense that he ceases to be an unregenerate man.

Since the old man is not the sinful disposition, consistency demands that the old man's counterpart, the new man, not be the new disposition. In light of what the old man is, *the new man is the regenerate man or the human person in his regenerate state*. As a new man, the saved person is characterized by freedom from the position of slave to the sinful disposition and by newness of life. Through resurrection with Christ (Romans 6:4-5) the person becomes a new man, for he is resurrected in the sense that he becomes a regenerate man. As a new man he possesses the new disposition.

The Evidence from Colossians 3:9-10

Consistency is not the only reason for concluding that the new disposition is not the new man. Colossians 3:9-10 provides evidence for the same conclusion. In Colossians 3:10 Paul declares that the new man experiences a renewal. This implies that the new man passes from a deficient to a better condition. By contrast, since the new disposition is an expression of the moral nature of God and since God's moral nature does not pass from a deficient to a better condition, then the new disposition does not pass from a deficient to a better condition. It never experiences a renewal. The fact that the new man experiences a renewal but the new disposition does not, indicates that the new man and the new disposition are not the same.

In light of what has been seen concerning the function of the new disposition within the regenerate man (Romans 7:14-25), it is evident that the new disposition is a major thing involved in effecting the renewal of the new man.

Conclusion

It can be concluded that the new man is not the new disposition. The new man is the regenerate man, but the new disposition is the law of God written in the heart of the regenerate man. Thus, the new disposition is in the new man, but it is not the new man.

The New Disposition and the Image of God and Christ

Transformation to the Image of God and Christ

While man had his favorable disposition toward God before the fall, the moral image of God in which man was created was uncorrupt. When man fell and replaced his favorable disposition with a disposition of enmity against God, the moral image of God was corrupted in man. These facts seem to indicate that man's disposition toward God has significant influence upon the moral image of God in man.

Paul teaches that the regenerate person is to be transformed to the moral image of God: "But we all, with unveiled face beholding as in a mirror the glory of the Lord, are being transformed into the same image from glory to glory, just as from the Lord, the Spirit" (2 Corinthians 3:18). Again he says: "The new man who is being renewed to a true knowledge according to the image of the One who created him" (Colossians 3:10).

Since Jesus Christ is "the image of the invisible God" (Colossians 1:15) and "the exact representation of His nature" (Hebrews 1:3), to be transformed to the moral image of God is to become like Jesus Christ. Paul definitely teaches that believers are to become like Christ, for he writes: "For whom He foreknew, He also predestined to become conformed to the image of His Son" (Romans 8:29). Thus, the moral image to which the believer is to be transformed is the image of God and Christ.

Since man's disposition toward God has significant influence upon the moral image of God in man, the new disposition which is favorable toward God must play a key role in the reversal of the corruption of the image of God and Christ in the believer.

The Progressive Nature of the Transformation

The transformation of the regenerate man to the moral image of God and Christ is not an instantaneous, once-for-all event. It is a gradual, step-by-step process throughout the life of the believer. That the transformation is a process is evident from what Paul says in 2 Corinthians 3:18: "We all . . . are being transformed into the same image from glory to glory." The language indicates that in the transformation the regenerate person passes from one stage of glory to another in a progressive movement forward. The process is emphasized again when Paul writes: "The new man who is being renewed to a true knowledge according to the image of the One who created him" (Colossians 3:10). The present tense of this statement indicates that the renewal is a process.

The process of transformation will not be completed until the believer sees Christ. John says: "Beloved, now we are children of God, and it has not appeared as yet what we shall be. We know that, when He appears, we shall be like Him, because we shall see Him just as He is" (1 John 3:2).

Putting together much of what has been seen thus far, the concept is this: at the moment of regeneration the person becomes the new man with the new disposition and the indwelling Holy Spirit. Although he is the new man with a new moral outlook, the regenerate person is not morally perfect as God is perfect. Because he still possesses the sinful disposition, he continues to be susceptible to its evil influence. For this reason he must go through a process of growth, being motivated by the new disposition and empowered by the Holy Spirit and winning one victory after another over the sinful disposition, until he is perfectly conformed to the image of God and Christ when he sees Christ.

Gutzke expresses it this way: "Christians start as *babes* and they grow to be in the fullness of the stature of the Lord Jesus Christ (Eph. 4:13). They are Christians all the while, but they grow. . . . But a Christian should never stop growing. From the time a person is born again, there should be growth."[2]

During this life, then, it is impossible to reach the perfection "to which the believer shall attain when he sees his blessed Lord as He is, 1 John iii.2. That Paul had not attained to this state of perfection, he in another place assures us, Phil. iii.12."[3]

Although perfection is impossible during this life, steady progress toward that final goal is to be made. The believer is to become more and more like Christ in his daily living.

The process of being transformed or renewed to the moral image of God has been called "sanctification" by theologians. Sauer writes: "The essence of sanctification is now to be found in the gradual transformation of man's character into the moral image of God."[4]

Conclusion

The new disposition plays a significant role in the transformation of the regenerate man to the moral image of God and Christ. As it works in the ways which Paul describes in Romans 7, it motivates the believer to become more and more Christlike in character and conduct.

10

THE NEW DISPOSITION AND 1 JOHN 3:9

The Statement of the Problem

ONE OF THE MOST DIFFICULT PASSAGES in the New Testament to interpret is 1 John 3:9. The reason for the difficulty is that in this passage John appears to contradict other statements of Scripture and actual Christian experience. He declares that those who have been begotten of God do not and cannot sin. In seeming contrast with this is the testimony of other Scriptures and Christian experience to the effect that believers actually do sin.

Inasmuch as the Scriptures do not contradict themselves and are true to Christian experience, how are John's statements in 1 John 3:9 to be interpreted?

Proposed Interpretations

All scholars agree that John's reference to those who have been begotten of God is a reference to those who have been regenerated by the Holy Spirit. They disagree, however, concerning the meaning of John's statements to the effect that the regenerate do not and cannot sin.

Some believe that John is teaching sinless perfection— the view that it is possible for a believer to come to a point in life in which he never sins again. This view has some problems. Firstly, this view suggests that not all believers attain sinless perfection during this life. By contrast, in 1 John 3:9 John declares that everyone who has been begotten (perfect tense) of God does not and cannot sin. If John is teaching the sinless perfection view, then he is saying that every Christian is sinlessly perfect.[1] Such teaching disagrees with the sinless perfection view.

Secondly, the sinless perfection view contradicts the rest of Scripture. Nowhere do the Scriptures indicate that any saint reached the point in life in which he never sinned again or became incapable of sinning. Even the Apostle Paul declared that he did not attain perfection prior to his upward call (Philippians 3:12-14).

Others believe that John is saying that the regenerate do not and cannot sin willfully and with knowledge.[2] This view has the problem of qualifying John's statements in ways that John does not.

Some are convinced that John means that it is impossible for the regenerate to become unregenerate again.[3] However, the language and context of 1 John 3:9 indicate that John is talking not about the state of a person but about practice or lack of practice that is the result of a state of existence.

Law contends that John is using the language of debate. While in the heat of argument with the Gnostics, John resorts to the use of exaggeration or absolutes in order to establish his point.[4] This view has a serious problem, for it implies that John, under the guise of truth, employs something which is not in complete accord with the truth. This is the same as saying that John resorts to a truthless means to attain a good end.

Lucke asserts that John is speaking ideally. John is stating what God has set as the ideal for the believer, but not what is true of the believer.[5] However, the language and context of 1 John 3:9 indicate that John is talking about actual practice, not about the ideal.

Some scholars believe that John is teaching that it is the new nature inside the believer that does not and cannot sin.

The problem with this view is that the context of 1 John 3:9 is talking about persons, not dispositions or natures, sinning and not sinning. In addition, the subject of the verb and infinitive for sinning in 1 John 3:9 is "no one who is born of God." Although the new nature is given through the new birth, it is the person himself (not the new nature) who is born or begotten of God. John says that it is the person who does not and cannot sin.

Several scholars believe that John is saying that although the believer can and does sin occasionally, he does not and cannot sin continuously as a habit of life. For several reasons the author is convinced that this is the correct view.

Firstly, John changes tenses between the verbs of 1 John 2:1 and those of 1 John 3:9. In 1 John 2:1, where John clearly talks about a believer committing an act of sin, the verbs which refer to the act of sin are aorist in tense. In 1 John 3:9 the verb and infinitive which refer to sinning are present in tense.[6] If John were referring to an act of sin in 1 John 3:9, consistency would demand that he use the aorist tense there as he does in 1 John 2:1. It appears that John purposely uses the present tense in 3:9 in order to present the idea of a continuous habit of sin.

Secondly, 1 John 3:7 indicates that the context of 3:9 deals with what is habitual, not with one act. In 3:7 John teaches that righteous action is evidence of a righteous nature. Certainly a righteous nature is not evidenced by only one act of righteousness. One act of righteousness opposed by habitual sinful acts is evidence of a sinful nature. It takes habitual acts of righteousness to demonstrate the possession of a righteous nature.

Thirdly, 1 John 3:8 also indicates that the context of 3:9 is dealing with that which is habitual. In 3:8 John asserts that the person who acts in the same sinful way as the devil is the offspring of or has the same sinful nature as the devil. He also indicates that the devil's sinful action is habitual; it is not limited to one act. The evidence for this is twofold. Firstly,

John says, "The devil sins [present tense] from the beginning" (literal translation). The combination of the present tense and the phrase "from the beginning" indicates habitual action. Secondly, John says that the Son of God appeared for the purpose of destroying the works (plural) of the devil. Since the devil sins habitually, the person who acts in the same sinful way as the devil must also sin habitually. Thus, John is declaring that it is the person who practices sin habitually who is the offspring of or has the same sinful nature as the devil.

The author is persuaded that John is teaching that every regenerate person does not and cannot sin habitually. Sinning is not the prevailing pattern or bent of the believer's life.

The Reason for the Sinlessness

The reason which John gives for the believer not sinning habitually is that "His seed abides in him." All scholars agree that John is talking about God's seed, but they disagree concerning the identification of "seed" and "him" in 1 John 3:9.

Some believe that "seed" refers to believers and that "him" refers to God. According to this view, John is saying that the "children of God [His seed] abide in Him."[7] For substantiation proponents of this view refer to 1 John 3:6 where John declares that everyone who abides in Christ does not sin.

Other scholars are convinced that "him" refers to the believer and that "seed" refers to something of God which abides in believers. According to this view, John is saying that the reason for the believer not sinning habitually is the fact that something of God abides in the believer.

The author is convinced of the latter view for the following reason: the major thrust of 1 John 3:9 is different from that of 3:6. The difference can be seen by placing the parallel statements of the two verses beside each other:

"No one who abides in Him sins" (3:6).

"No one who is born of God practices sin" (3:9). The

major thrust of 1 John 3:6 is that abiding in Christ determines practice. By contrast the major thrust of 3:9 is that fatherhood determines practice.[8] In 1 John 3:8-10 John presents the practical effect that God and Satan have upon their offspring. In 3:8 John asserts that it is the offspring of the devil who sins habitually. By contrast in 3:9 he declares that it is the offspring of God who does not sin habitually. In 3:10 he says that the distinction between the offspring of God and the offspring of Satan is made obvious by the difference in their practice. It is obvious that John is emphasizing the concept that fatherhood determines practice.

Since the major thrust of 1 John 3:9 differs from the major thrust of 3:6, the author is convinced that that which "abides" in 3:9 must also differ from that which "abides" in 3:6. Since it is the believer who "abides" in 3:6, it must not be the believer which "abides" in 3:9. That which abides in 3:9 must be something of God within the believer.

Among those scholars who believe that "seed" in 1 John 3:9 refers to something of God which abides in believers there is disagreement concerning what that something of God is. Some believe that it is the word of God.[9] They refer to Matthew 13:1-23 where Jesus, making use of an analogy from agriculture, portrays the word of God as seed that is sown.

The author rejects this view because of the context. In 1 John 3:9 the seed in question does not correspond to the seed involved in agriculture. Instead it corresponds to the seed of a father involved in human generation.[10] The verse talks about the person who is begotten of God.

Other scholars are convinced that "seed" refers to the Holy Spirit.[11] They argue that, since the Holy Spirit is the divine agent of regeneration, He must be the seed which abides in the regenerate.

The author does not accept this view, for in the analogy of human generation the seed which is implanted is not a person. Instead, it is implanted by a person. Inasmuch as the Holy Spirit is a person, He is the agent who implants God's seed in human beings. He is not the seed itself.

Some scholars regard the seed to be the germ of the new, divine, spiritual life which is implanted in human persons by the Holy Spirit at the time of regeneration.[12] Some who hold to this view identify the seed further as a holy disposition,[13] God's nature,[14] the ruling principle of the believer's growth,[15] and a new nature.[16] Law expresses it this way: "As the human parent once for all imparts his own nature to his offspring, so, in virtue of the Divine Begetting, the Divine nature is permanently imparted to the children of God."[17]

The author accepts this view as the correct one. He is convinced that the "seed" of 1 John 3:9 is the new disposition implanted in a person by the Holy Spirit at the time of regeneration. There are several reasons for this conviction. Firstly, in the analogy of human generation one of the things which is involved in the implantation of the human father's seed is the impartation of the father's sinful disposition to the child who is procreated. Since the implantation of seed involves the impartation of the father's disposition to the child, it can be concluded that the implantation of God's seed involves the impartation of His holy disposition to His child.

Secondly, this view of the seed corresponds with what was seen earlier in 2 Peter 1:4 where Peter states that believers are partakers of the divine nature. In the treatment of that passage it was demonstrated that believers partake of God's nature in one respect: they partake of His holy disposition as a result of the Holy Spirit placing it in them at the time of regeneration.

Thirdly, this view corresponds best with the major thrust of 1 John 3:9. As noted earlier, the major thrust of that verse is that fatherhood determines practice. Surely the manner in which fatherhood determines practice is that in the act of begetting the father imparts his disposition to his child through the implantation of his seed. There is no better way that John could have developed the major thrust of 3:9 than to teach that everyone who has been begotten of God does not sin habitually because God's holy disposition abides in this begotten one. The believer does not possess God's disposition temporarily. He possesses it continuously and forever.

Conclusion

The author has concluded that John teaches the following in 1 John 3:9: the regenerate person does not and cannot sin habitually, because God's holy disposition which is opposed to sin remains in that person. This disposition (the new disposition) is the seed from which the believer's new, righteous way of life springs forth and grows.

11

THE NEW DISPOSITION
AND THE OLD TESTAMENT SAINT

The Problem of the Old Testament Saint

IN JEREMIAH 31:31-34 God promised His Old Testament people that in the future, when He would establish the new covenant, He would write His law in human hearts. This was His way of promising the new disposition in conjunction with the new covenant. It was noted earlier that the new covenant was not established during Old Testament times. Does this mean that God never wrote His law in human hearts during Old Testament times? To put it another way: does this mean that the Old Testament saint did not possess the new disposition?

The New Disposition in Old Testament Times

The author is convinced that the new disposition was given to Old Testament saints in spite of the fact that those saints were not under the new covenant. This conviction is based upon several lines of evidence which will be examined now.

The Regeneration of the Old Testament Saint

Earlier it was noted that the new disposition is imparted to a person through the Holy Spirit's work of regeneration. This means that, if Old Testament saints were regenerated, then surely they possessed the new disposition.

That Old Testament saints were regenerated is evident for several reasons. Firstly, Jesus told Nicodemus that the only way into the kingdom of God is through regeneration (John 3:3,5), and yet Jesus said that Abraham, Isaac, Jacob, and the prophets belong to the kingdom of God (Luke 13:28-29).[1] It is obvious from this that Abraham, Isaac, Jacob, and the prophets, all of whom were Old Testament saints, were regenerated.

Secondly, the acts of faith performed by such Old Testament saints as Noah, Abraham, David, Moses, and others indicate that these men were spiritually alive. But spiritual life comes only as a result of regeneration.[2] The fact that these men were spiritually alive indicates that as Old Testament saints they were regenerated.

From this it is evident that Old Testament saints were regenerated and thereby possessed the new disposition.

Isaiah 51:7

Through the Prophet Isaiah God said to a segment of the people of Israel: "Listen to Me, you who know righteousness, a people in whose heart is My law: Do not fear the reproach of man, neither be dismayed at their revilings" (Isaiah 51:7).

Scholars are agreed that God is addressing a remnant or nucleus of Israelites who were truly regenerate, who know righteousness by personal experience and who had the law of God in their hearts.[3] Since the new disposition consists of the law of God in the heart, it can be concluded that these Old Testament saints possessed the new disposition and put its impulses into practice.

Statements in the Psalms

In the psalms David makes statements which indicate that both he and other Israelites had the law of God in their hearts. In Psalm 37:31 David describes the righteous man as follows: "The law of his God is in his heart; his steps do not slip." In Psalm 40:8 he writes: "I delight to do Thy will, O my God; Thy Law is within my heart." Since the new disposition consists of the law of God in the heart, these passages make it obvious that David and other Old Testament saints did possess the new disposition. It is interesting to note how similar the statement in Psalm 40:8 is to statements made by Paul as a regenerate man in Romans 7:14-22.

The Concluding Question

The fact that Old Testament saints had the new disposition gives rise to a question: if Old Testament saints living under the old covenant possessed the new disposition the same as saints living under the new covenant, then what is so new or special about God's promise to give the new disposition in conjunction with the new covenant?

The new or special thing about God's promise is this: through His promise God was committing Himself in the future to give the new disposition to Israelites *as part of a divine covenant with Israel.* God did not mean to imply by His promise that He never gave the new disposition to people prior to the establishment of the new covenant. Indeed, He did give it to every genuine Old Testament believer, but He did not give it to them as part of a covenant with Israel.

Although Old Testament Israelite saints had the law of God in their hearts while living under the old covenant, they did not have that new disposition *because* they were under that covenant. The old covenant did not guarantee that everyone living under it would be regenerated. In fact regeneration wasn't even provided by that covenant. Every Israelite came into old covenant relationship with God by virtue of two things: physical birth to Israelite parents, and circumcision (if a male). But not every Israelite was regenerated. Thus, many Israelites who were in old covenant relationship with God were unregenerate people without the new disposition. Although the old covenant demanded that the Israelites have the law of God in their hearts (Deuteronomy 6:5-6), it did not provide that new disposition for them.

In contrast with this, the new covenant guarantees that everyone living under it has the law of God in the heart, for one of the main things it provides is the new disposition. No one can come into new covenant relationship with God except through regeneration. Thus, everyone in the new covenant relationship with God is regenerated and has the new disposition. In the future, when the nation of Israel is under the new covenant, each Israelite under the new covenant will have the new disposition *because* of his being under that covenant.

The new thing about God's promise in Jeremiah 31:31-34 is that in the future God will give the new disposition to Israelites as part of His divine covenant with the nation. This He did not do in the past.

12

THE NEW DISPOSITION
AND THE OLD COVENANT LAW

The Statement of the Problem

IN ROMANS 6:14 Paul says to Christians: "You are not under law, but under grace." Earlier it was noted that Paul includes all aspects, even the moral aspect, of the external, old covenant law in the expression "not under law." In light of this, some scholars teach that Paul is saying that Christians are not under the moral aspect of the old covenant law, even as a rule of life or means of sanctification.

Other scholars react negatively to this teaching. They assert that there are only two alternatives open to the Christian: either to be under the moral aspect of the old covenant law as a rule of life or to be lawless. They brand as error the view that Christians are not under any aspect of the old covenant law. Some call that view "antinomianism."[1]

This difference of opinion indicates the existence of a problem: if the Christian is under no aspect of the old covenant law, then what is there to prevent the Christian from being lawless?

The Proposed Solution to the Problem

In light of what has been learned in this study, the author proposes that the solution to the problem is found in the new disposition and the Holy Spirit. Because the law of God has been written in his heart and the power of the Holy Spirit has been made available to him, the Christian does not need any aspect of the external old covenant law to motivate and enable him to live a holy life. Because the new disposition causes the believer to concur joyfully with the will of God and to will to do the will of God, and because the Holy Spirit empowers him to do the will of God, the Christian need not be under the old covenant law in order to avoid being lawless. In other words, the new disposition and the Holy Spirit provide a third alternative to the Christian: that of being freed totally from every aspect of the old covenant law without being lawless.

Those who recognize only two alternatives overlook an important truth: the old covenant law was only one way for God to administer His eternal holy precepts. Because God's moral absolutes are an expression of His eternal, changeless, holy nature, the moral absolutes themselves are eternal and changeless. They have always existed. They existed long before the old covenant law was established, and they continue to exist since the old covenant law was abolished. Although God's moral absolutes are eternal and changeless, they have been administered by God in different ways at different times in history. The old covenant law was only one way for God to administer His moral absolutes to one group of people (the nation of Israel) during one period of history. Thus, the fact that the Christian is not under any aspect of the old covenant law does not mean that he is divorced from the moral absolutes of God. What it does mean is that the Christian is divorced from that particular way for God to administer His moral absolutes.

Through the old covenant, God's absolutes were administered externally in the form of an external law. This is not to say that that was the only way in which they were administered while the old covenant was in effect. To Old Testament saints God's holy precepts were also administered internally even while the old covenant was in effect for, as seen earlier, Old Testament saints had the new disposition within them. But these saints obtained this internal administration of God's precepts through some means other than the old covenant. The old covenant itself provided only the external adminis-tration.

In contrast with the old covenant administration, through grace God's holy precepts are administered internally in the form of a holy disposition which consists of the law of God written in the heart. Since the regenerate are the only ones who possess this holy disposition, it can be concluded that the regenerate are the only subjects of this internal administra-tion. Because the administration through grace is inward in nature, the Christian is not *under* the law of God. Instead of the law being *over* him, it is *in* him as part of him.

Thus, although the Christian is not under the old cove-nant administration of God's moral precepts, he is as respon-sible to those precepts as was any subject of the old covenant administration. The difference is that the Christian operates under a different administration of those precepts. He is under the grace administration rather than the old covenant administration (Romans 6:14). The Christian, then, can be free from the old covenant law without being lawless.

The Scriptural Evidence for the Solution

Several passages of Scripture indicate that Christians can be free from the old covenant law without being lawless.

Romans 7:4,6

Paul writes:

Therefore, my brethren, you also were made to die to the Law through the body of Christ, that you might be joined to another, to Him who was raised from the dead, that we might bear fruit for

God . . . . But now we have been released from the Law, having died to that by which we were bound, so that we serve in newness of the Spirit and not in oldness of the letter (Romans 7:4,6).

In the earlier treatment of these verses it was noted that the context indicates that the "law" to which Paul refers is the entire old covenant law, including even its moral aspect.

Inasmuch as death involves the separation of two things, it can be concluded that, when Paul talks about Christians having died to the "law," he is teaching that Christians have been separated from the "law." Since the "law" in these verses is the old covenant law in its entirety, it can be concluded that Paul is asserting that Christians have been separated from every aspect of the old covenant law, even from its moral aspect.

The separation of the Christian from the old covenant law is indicated in another way in Romans 7:6. There Paul says Christians "have been released from the Law." The verb "released" means "to take from the sphere of operation."[2] The assertion is that Christians have been removed from the old covenant law's sphere of operation. To put it another way, they have been removed from the old covenant's external administration of God's moral precepts.

The fact that Christians can be separated from the old covenant law without being lawless is indicated by Paul in two ways. Firstly, in Romans 7:4 he teaches that the ultimate purpose for Christians being separated from the old covenant law is that they "might bear fruit for God." Thus, instead of separation from the "law" being directed to the negative end of lawlessness, for the Christian it is directed to the positive end of holy living.

Secondly, in Romans 7:6 Paul declares that the result of Christians being separated from the old covenant law is that they "serve in newness of the Spirit and not in oldness of the letter." Instead of the separation resulting in lawlessness, it results in service to God. Granted, it is service in the sphere of an administration that is different from that of the old covenant, but it is still service to God. When verse 6 was treated earlier it was concluded that the "newness" of the Spirit involved the new disposition and the power of the Holy Spirit.

Thus, in Romans 7:4,6 Paul is teaching that Christians have been separated from the old covenant law, but this separation has a holy life as its purpose and service to God as its result. Because of the new disposition and the power of the Holy Spirit, Christians can be separated from the old covenant law without being lawless.

1 Timothy 1:8-10

Paul declares:

But we know that the Law is good, if one uses it lawfully, realizing the fact that law is not made for a righteous man, but for those who are lawless and rebellious, for the ungodly and sinners, for the unholy and profane, for those who kill their fathers or mothers, for murderers and immoral men and homosexuals and kidnappers and liars and perjurers, and whatever else is contrary to sound teaching (1 Timothy 1:8-10).

A few scholars believe that Paul is not talking about the old covenant law in this passage. They base this belief upon two things: the fact that the word "law" in verse 9 has no article before it, and the claim that the people mentioned in verses 9 and 10 must be heathen, not Jews.[3]

The author is not convinced of this view on the basis of these two items. Concerning the second item, surely there existed among the Jews the kind of people mentioned in 1 Timothy 1:9-10. The old covenant law instructed the Jews concerning the treatment of such people within the nation. The Old Testament records examples of such people within the nation. Paul in Romans 2—3 indicates that the Jews were no better morally than the Gentiles.

With regard to the first item, Kent gives reasons for believing that Paul has the old covenant law in mind in 1 Timothy 1:9. Firstly, the preceding context discusses would-be law teachers who certainly were exponents of the old covenant law. They were a problem to the church at Ephesus. Secondly, in verse 8 the word "law" does have the article. Thirdly, the list of sins that belong to the kind of people mentioned in verses 9-10 follow the order of the Ten Commandments.[4]

For these reasons the author is convinced that in this passage Paul is talking about the old covenant law. He was interested to find that almost all the scholars consulted on this issue are convinced of the same. The very fact that Paul follows the order of the Ten Commandments in 1 Timothy 1:9-10 indicates that he is talking about even the moral aspect of the old covenant law.

Paul's statement to the effect that "the Law is good, if one uses it lawfully" implies there is a right way and a wrong way to use the old covenant law, including the Ten Commandments.

The fact that there is a right way and a wrong way to use the old covenant law gives rise to a question. What is the right way and what is the wrong way to use that law?

The author, together with every scholar consulted, is convinced that Paul answers this question in 1 Timothy 1:9-10. He claims that the old covenant law was made, not for the righteous, but for the lawless and their kind. A comparison of 1 Timothy 1:9-10 with 1 Corinthians 6:9-10 indicates that the lawless and their kind are the unregenerate. If they are the unregenerate, then the "righteous" must be the regenerate. Paul is saying, then, that the old covenant law, including the Ten Commandments, was made, not for the regenerate, but for the unregenerate.

In light of this claim of Paul, the answer to the question concerning the right way and the wrong way to use the old covenant law is as follows: since the old covenant law was made for the unregenerate, it is right to put the unregenerate under that law. But since the old covenant law, including the Ten Commandmants, was not made for the regenerate, it is wrong to put the regenerate under that law, even under its moral aspect.

Every scholar consulted by the author was convinced that the old covenant law was made to be directed against lawlessness. The context of 1 Timothy 1:8-10 indicates that this is so.

Since the old covenant law was made to be directed against lawlessness, since that law was not made for the regenerate, and since it is wrong to put the regenerate under that law, it can be concluded that the regenerate are not lawless. Even apart from the old covenant law with its Ten Commandments, the regenerate are not lawless.

On the basis of 1 Timothy 1:8-10, then, it can be concluded that Christians can be free from the old covenant law without being lawless.

Galatians 5:18

In Galatians 5:18 Paul says: "But if you are led by the Spirit, you are not under the Law."

The context of this passage makes it obvious that the law that Paul has in mind is the old covenant law. Paul is combating the Judaizers who had been trying to convince the Galatian Christians that they must choose between a life of lawlessness and a life governed by the old covenant law.

The context (Galatians 5:19-21) also implies that Paul is thinking primarily of the moral aspect of the old covenant law. It is the moral aspect that is opposed to such things as immorality, idolatry, and envyings.

To be led by the Spirit must involve more than guidance or the pointing out of the right way by the Holy Spirit, for the old covenant law gave such guidance, but Paul sets the Spirit in contrast with the law. To be led by the Spirit must include the controlling power of the Holy Spirit.

Since the Judaizers had been teaching the Christians that there were only two alternatives open to them and since Paul is combating their teaching, one is forced to conclude that Paul is presenting a third alternative: to be controlled by the power of the Holy Spirit.

Paul is saying that those who are controlled by the power of the Holy Spirit are not under the old covenant law. The context teaches that to be controlled by the power of the Spirit is not to be lawless (Galatians 5:16-17,22-23). Thus, it is possible for the Christian to be free from the old covenant law, even its moral aspect, without being lawless.

Galatians 5:22-23

In this passage Paul declares: "But the fruit of the Spirit is love, joy, peace, patience, kindness, goodness, faithfulness, gentleness, self-control; against such things there is no law."

This passage appears in the same context as Galatians 5:18. In fact, it is part of the same argument that Paul deals with in Galatians 5:18. On the basis of these factors two things can be concluded. Firstly, the law that Paul refers to in 5:23 must be the old covenant law including its moral aspect. Secondly, the fruit of the Spirit listed in 5:22-23 must be the result of the controlling power of the Holy Spirit.

Paul's statement in this passage is very significant in light of what he teaches in Galatians 5:18: that those who are controlled by the power of the Holy Spirit are not under the old covenant law. In 5:22-23 it appears that he gives the reason why those who are controlled by the Spirit are not under the law. It is because the Spirit produces so much righteous fruit in the lives of those whom He controls that no external law is necessary to be directed against their actions.

Paul's statement in this passage is very significant in light of what he teaches in 1 Timothy 1:8-10. As noted earlier, in 1 Timothy 1:8-10 Paul asserts that the old covenant law was not made for the righteous or regenerate. Instead, it was made to oppose the lawlessness of the unregenerate. The implication is that the external old covenant law is not neces- sary to oppose the righteousness of the regenerate.

In essence Paul is teaching the same thing in Galatians 5:22-23 as in 1 Timothy 1:8-10. In Galatians he is saying that the controlling power of the Holy Spirit produces righteous fruit in the Christian. Since this fruit is righteous by nature, it is not necessary to have the external old covenant law to oppose it.

In light of Paul's teaching, the following can be con- cluded from Galatians 5:22-23: since the power of the Holy Spirit can produce in the Christian the kind of righteousness that makes the old covenant law unnecessary, it is possible for the Christian to be free from the old covenant law without being lawless.

1 Corinthians 9:20-21

In the midst of statements concerning the relationship of Christian liberty to his ministry Paul says:

And to the Jews I became as a Jew, that I might win Jews; to those who are under the Law, as under the Law, though not being myself under the Law, that I might win those who are under the Law; to those who are without law, as without law, though not being with- out the law of God but under the law of Christ, that I might win those who are without law (1 Corinthians 9:20-21).

In 1 Corinthians 9:20 Paul plainly states that he himself was not under "the Law." In this verse "the Law" is the law that the Jews were under. Inasmuch as the law that the Jews were under was the old covenant law, Paul must be saying that he himself was not under the old covenant law.

In 1 Corinthians 9:21 Paul indicates that occasionally he practiced some aspects of Gentile culture when with unbeliev- ing Gentiles. Paul knows that this practice, together with the truth that he is not under the old covenant law, exposes him to the charge of lawlessness. For this reason he hastens to add: "Though not being without the law of God but under the law of Christ."

In this statement Paul uses two contrasting terms. The one is translated "without the law." The other is translated "under the law." The basic meaning of the first term is "lawless."[5] Thus, Paul is saying that, although he is not under the old covenant law, he is not lawless with reference to God.

The second term appears only one other time in the New Testament. In Acts 19:39 it refers either to a "lawful [assembly] in contrast to a mob [or to a] regular [assembly] in contrast to one called for a special occasion."[6] Between the meanings of "lawful" and "regular," only "lawful" is appropriate to the context of 1 Corinthians 9:21.

The second term also means "righteous" or "upright" when used of persons.[7] This meaning is appropriate to the context of 1 Corinthians 9:21 and agrees with the concept of "lawful." It appears, then, that Paul is saying that he is lawful, righteous, or upright with reference to Christ.

On the basis of what has been seen earlier concerning the law of God in the heart (the new disposition) and the law of the Spirit of life in Christ Jesus (Romans 8:2) dwelling and working within the Christian to produce the holy character of Christ, the author wonders if these are the things which Paul had in mind when he chose to use the second term. The second term is made up of two words which mean "in" and "law." It appears that Paul is saying that he is "in-lawed" with reference to Christ. Did Paul purposely use this word in order to stress the internal relationship which the Christian has with Christ through the new disposition and the controlling power of the Holy Spirit?

In 1 Corinthians 9:20-21 Paul is saying that, although he himself is not under the old covenant law, he is not lawless with reference to God. Instead, he is "in-lawed" with reference to Christ. This means that he is lawful or righteous with reference to Christ. Since Paul speaks as a Christian, it can be concluded that it is possible for a Christian to be free from the old covenant law without being lawless.

Titus 2:11-14

For the grace of God has appeared, bringing salvation to all men, instructing us to deny ungodliness and worldly desires and to live sensibly, righteously, and godly in the present age, looking for the blessed hope and the appearing of the glory of our great God and Saviour, Christ Jesus; who gave Himself for us, that He might redeem us from every lawless deed and purify for Himself a people for His own possession, zealous for good deeds (Titus 2:11-14).

Paul is saying that the grace of God teaches the Christian to deny a sinful life and to live a righteous life. In light of what Paul says in Romans 6:14 to the effect that Christians are not under law but under grace, this Titus 2 passage is quite significant. It shows that there is something to prevent the Christian from being lawless while being free from the old covenant law. That something is the grace of God.

Earlier it was noted that being under the grace of God involves the possession of the new disposition and the Holy Spirit for the Christian. As the new disposition causes the Christian to will to do the will of God and as the Holy Spirit empowers him to do that will, the Christian denies the lawless way of life and lives the righteous way of life. This is what is involved in grace teaching the Christian.

Since the grace of God is able to overcome sin and to produce righteousness in the Christian, there is no need for the Christian to be under any aspect of the old covenant law. Because of the grace of God, the Christian can be free from the old covenant law without being lawless.

A Concluding Question

It has been demonstrated that one reason why the Christian is not under the old covenant law is the fact that he possesses the new disposition. In addition, it has been demonstrated that Old Testament saints also had the new disposition. Although Old Testament saints had the new disposition, they continued to live under the external old covenant law. The combination of these factors gives rise to a question: if Christians are not under the old covenant law because they possess the new disposition, then why did Old Testament saints continue to live under that law with the new disposition?

The answer to the question is found in the fact that in Old Testament times Israel's national government was a theocracy. Because every national government has unregenerate people living under its dominion and because unregenerate people are lawless by nature, it is necessary for every national government to have an external law system directed against lawlessness (Romans 13:1-4). Each government sets its laws in authority over all its citizens, regenerate as well as unregenerate. Israel was no exception to this fact. Because Israel's government was a theocracy, its external, national law was the divine law given to it at Mount Sinai. Thus, although Old Testament saints possessed the new disposition, they continued to live under the external, old covenant law because it was also the law of their nation's government.

During the present dispensation there is no nation with a God-ordained, theocratic government. Although God establishes every governmental authority (Romans 13:1) and although some governments have some laws that are based upon God's moral absolutes, no government of this age has received its external law system by direct revelation from God as Israel did. For this reason God calls the governments of this age "every human institution" (1 Peter 2:13). Their laws are human, not divine, in origin.

Christians do live under the authority of the external laws of their national governments (Romans 13:1-7; 1 Peter 2:13), but because no government today is a theocracy, no Christian is living under the laws of the external old covenant law.

CONCLUSION

Things Learned from This Study

THROUGH THE COURSE of this study numerous things have been learned concerning the new nature. Firstly, the new nature is not the unique combination of attributes which determines that a man is a human being in contrast with all other kinds of beings or things. Instead, it is a disposition. Because this is so, its reception by a human being does not involve a metaphysical change in that person.

Secondly, the reception of the new nature became necessary because man lost his original, favorable disposition toward God and became thoroughly confirmed in a disposition of enmity against God through Adam's first sin. Because of this great spiritual change in man, every part of his being became enslaved to sin. The sinful disposition gained the position of master over man. Man needed a new disposition or nature which would be confirmed and favorable toward God.

Thirdly, in such Old Testament prophetic passages as Jeremiah 31:31-34, Ezekiel 36:25-28, and 11:19-20 God promised to give such a new nature to Israelites in conjunction with the new covenant. This new nature was to be given on the basis of the forgiveness of sins. It would consist of the law of God written in the heart and would be imparted through the regenerating work of the Holy Spirit. As the result of it and the Holy Spirit being placed together inside a person, that person would know God in an experiential way and would do the will of God.

Fourthly, the new nature is not the same thing as the work of the law in Gentile hearts mentioned by Paul in Romans 2:14-15. It is superior to what the unregenerate Gentiles have; it is more than an inherent moral consciousness.

Fifthly, the new nature is not produced in man through a reformation of the old nature or sinful disposition. It is not something that grows or develops in a person over a period of time. It cannot be gotten through human effort. Instead, it is imparted to a person instantaneously through the supernatural work of the Holy Spirit called regeneration or the new birth. It constitutes the moral nature of God planted in man. Only regenerate people possess the new nature.

Sixthly, Christians or saints of the present dispensation possess the new nature.

Seventhly, as the result of the believer experiencing a death with Christ, the sinful disposition loses permanently its position of master over him, and the believer loses permanently his position of slave under the sinful disposition.

Eighthly, although the sinful disposition will never hold the position of master over the believer again, it continues with him for the rest of his life and tries to exercise its controlling power over him. Because this is so, the believer is confronted with a continuing conflict against the power of the sinful disposition. In this conflict the new nature does several things for the believer: it causes him to agree with, to serve, to joyfully concur with, and to will to do the will of God in his inner self. It does not, however, provide the believer with the power necessary to overcome the power of the sinful disposition, and therefore, to do the will of God. The Christian needs more than the new nature in order to do God's will.

If the believer relies upon the old covenant law as the source of power necessary to overcome the power of the sinful disposition, the believer will be defeated by the sinful disposition, for the old covenant law does not give power. It abandons the believer to his own self-effort.

Ninthly, the believer is not doomed to a permanent state of defeat, however, for the grace of God also gives the believer the Holy Spirit to dwell within. The Holy Spirit is related to the believer's new nature in two ways. Firstly, the Holy Spirit is the agent whom Christ uses to place the new nature inside the believer. Secondly, the Holy Spirit is the powerful ally of the new nature inside the believer. At the time of regeneration the Holy Spirit set the believer free from the controlling power of the sinful disposition and made available the power necessary to overcome the power of the sinful disposition and, therefore, to do God's will. If the believer relies upon the grace of God to give him victory, the Holy Spirit will enable the new nature to govern more than the will. He will enable it to govern the whole person.

Tenthly, the "new nature" is not the "new man" referred to by Paul in Colossians 3:9-10. The "new man" is the regenerate man or the human person in his regenerate state. As a new man, the saved person is characterized by freedom from the position of slave to the sinful disposition and by newness of life. The new nature is in the new man, but it is not the new man.

Eleventhly, the new nature plays a significant role in the transformation of the regenerate man to the moral image of God and Christ. As it works in the ways which Paul describes in Romans 7, it motivates the believer to become more and more Christlike in character and conduct. This motivation will continue until the believer attains moral perfection when he sees Christ.

Twelfthly, in 1 John 3:9 John teaches that the regenerate person does not and cannot sin habitually, because God's holy disposition that is opposed to sin remains in that person. This disposition (the new disposition) is the seed from which the believer's new, righteous way of life springs forth and grows.

Thirteenthly, the new nature was given to the Old Testament saint even though Old Testament saints did not live under the new covenant. It was not given *because* the Old Testament saint was under the old covenant, for the old covenant did not provide for the bestowal of the new nature. Instead, it was given through the grace of God totally apart from any provision of the old covenant.

Fourteenthly, the grace of God makes it possible for the Christian or believer of the present dispensation to be free from every aspect of the old covenant law without being lawless. As a result of providing the Christian with the new nature and the power of the Holy Spirit, the grace of God is able to produce in and through the Christian the kind of righteousness that the old covenant law demanded but could not produce. The grace of God is able to produce this without the Christian being under the external old covenant law.

The Reception of the New Nature

This study was written primarily for the benefit of believers. It may be, however, that you, the present reader, are not a Christian. You have never placed your trust in Jesus Christ, the Son of God, to be your personal Saviour from sin. If that be the case, then you do not possess the new nature or the Holy Spirit. As a result, you do not have the equipment necessary to live a godly life.

In order to become a Christian and receive the new nature and Holy Spirit, you must honestly admit that you have sinned against God, that you thereby stand condemned before Him, and that you need a Saviour from the penalty of your sin. In addition, you must genuinely believe that Jesus Christ is the Son of God, that He died on the cross for your sins, that He was buried, and that He rose bodily from the dead on the third day after His death. As the culmination of your faith, you must personally trust Jesus Christ (not your works, not baptism, not communion, not your membership in a church or any other organization) to save you from the penalty of your sin. At the moment you do this the Holy Spirit will make you a "new man" (will regenerate you), will place the new nature within you, and will indwell you. Why not do this now?

NOTES

Chapter 1—Basic Definitions

1. William F. Arndt and F. Wilbur Gingrich, *A Greek-English Lexicon of the New Testament,* p. 877.
2. Joseph Henry Thayer, *A Greek-English Lexicon of the New Testament,* p. 661.
3. James Hope Moulton and George Milligan, *The Vocabulary of the Greek Testament,* p. 679.
4. Henry George Liddell and Robert Scott, *A Greek-English Lexicon,* p. 1965.
5. Charles Hodge, *Commentary on the Epistle to the Romans,* p. 55.
6. Taken from *The Zondervan Pictorial Bible Dictionary,* edited by Merrill C. Tenney. Copyright 1963, 1964, 1967 by Zondervan Publishing House, p. 573. Used by permission.
7. Charlton T. Lewis and Charles Short, "natura," in *Latin Dictionary,* p. 1189.
8. "nature," *The Oxford English Dictionary,* 1961, VII, 41.
9. By permission. From *Webster's Third New International Dictionary,* copyright 1981 by Merriam-Webster Inc., publisher of the Merriam-Webster Dictionaries.
10. "Nature," *The American College Dictionary,* 1948, text ed. p. 810. By permission from the American College Dictionary,© 1970 by Random House, Inc.
11. Taken from *A Systematic Theology of the Christian Religion,* Vol. I, 251, by James Oliver Buswell. Copyright 1962 by Zondervan Publishing House. Used by permission.
12. *What, Then, Is Man?* p. 52 (original source not available to author).
13. *Ibid.,* p. 67.

Chapter 2—THE DISPOSITIONS OF MAN BEFORE AND AFTER
THE FALL

1. Edward J. Young, *Genesis 3*, p. 70.
2. Augustus Hopkins Strong, *Systematic Theology*, pp. 516-17.
3. Young, *Genesis 3*, p. 47.
4. Taken from *A Systematic Theology of the Christian Religion*, Vol. I, 276-277, by James Oliver Buswell. Copyright 1962 by Zonder-van Publishing House. Used by permission.
5. L. Berkhof, *Systematic Theology*, p. 222.
6. Cornelius Van Til, *The Defense of the Faith*, p. 63.
7. *Ibid.*, p. 178.
8. *Ibid.*, p. 179.
9. *Ibid.*, p. 187.
10. Berkhof, *Systematic Theology*, 246.
11. Walther Eichrodt, *Theology of the Old Testament*, II, 389.
12. *Ibid.*, p. 132.
13. Young, *Genesis 3*, p. 47.
14. Van Til, *The Defense of the Faith*, p. 63.
15. Fred H. Klooster, "The Nature of Man," in *Christian Faith and Modern Theology*, p. 152.
16. Berkhof, *Systematic Theology*, pp. 225-26.
17. John A. T. Robinson, *The Body*, p. 19.
18. John Murray, "The Epistle to the Romans," Vol. I, in *The New International Commentary on the New Testament*, p. 286.
19. Robert Haldane, *Exposition of the Epistle to the Romans*, p. 333.
20. *Ibid.*, p. 334.
21. Murray, *The Epistle to the Romans*, I, 286.
22. *Ibid.*, I, 287.
23. Berkhof, *Systematic Theology*, p. 221.
24. Eichrodt, *Theology of the Old Testament*, II, 387.
25. *Ibid.*, II, 411.

Chapter 3—THE NEW DISPOSITION AND OLD TESTAMENT
PROPHECY

1. E. Henderson, *The Book of the Prophet Jeremiah and That of the Lamentations*, p. 190.

2. Theo. Laetsch, *Jeremiah*, p. 256.
3. A. W. Streane, *The Book of the Prophet Jeremiah Together with the Lamentations,* of *The Cambridge Bible for Schools and Colleges,* p. 28.
4. *Ibid.,* p. 106.
5. Laetsch, *Jeremiah*, p. 161.
6. Robert Jamieson, A. R. Fausset, and David Brown, *A Commentary, Critical, Experimental, and Practical, on the Old and New Testaments,* Vol. IV: Jeremiah-Malachi, p. 111.
7. Henry Cowles, *Jeremiah, and His Lamentations,* p. 243.
8. A. C. Gaebelein, *The Annotated Bible,* Jeremiah, p. 191; *Gaebelein's Concise Commentary on the Whole Bible,* p. 575.
9. John Calvin, *Commentaries on the Book of the Prophet Jeremiah and the Lamentations,* IV, 131.
10. Norman C. Habel, "Jeremiah, Lamentations," of *Concordia Commentary,* p. 246.
11. Charles Bridges, *An Exposition of Proverbs,* p. 53.
12. Walther Eichrodt, *Theology of the Old Testament,* II, 144.
13. Johannes Behm, "kardia," *Theological Dictionary of the New Testament,* Vol. III, p. 612.
14. F. F. Bruce "The Epistle to the Hebrews," of *The New International Commentary on the New Testament,* p. 172.
15. *Ibid.,* pp. 172-73.
16. W. H. Bennett, "The Book of Jeremiah," of *The Expositor's Bible,* p. 352.
17. *Ibid.,* p. 353.
18. Habel, *Jeremiah*, p. 247.
19. E. W. Hengstenberg, *Christology of the Old Testament,* II, p. 440.
20. Matthew Henry, *Matthew Henry's Commentary on the Whole Bible,* Vol. IV: "Jeremiah to Malachi," n.p.
21. James Comper Gray, *The Biblical Museum,* IV, 120.
22. W. F. Adeney, "Jeremiah," by T. K. Cheyne and W. F. Adeney, of *The Pulpit Commentary,* p. 26.
23. Bruce, *Hebrews*, p. 174.
24. C. F. Keil, "The Prophecies of Jeremiah," in *Biblical Commentary on the Old Testament,* II, 40.
25. Laetsch, *Jeremiah*, p. 257.
26. Adeney, *Jeremiah*, p. 26.
27. Calvin, *Jeremiah*, IV, 130.

28. Laetsch, *Jeremiah,* p. 257.

29. *Ibid.*

30. Walther Eichrodt, *Ezekiel,* pp. 497-98.

31. Charles Lee Feinberg, *The Prophecy of Ezekiel,* p. 209.

32. Eichrodt, *Theology of the Old Testament,* II, 131.

33. S. Lewis Johnson, "A Survey of Biblical Psychology in the Epistle to the Romans" (unpublished Th.D. dissertation), p. 76.

34. Elmer Towns, "The Meaning of Heart in the New Testament," 41.

35. H. L. Ellison, *Ezekiel: The Man and His Message,* p. 128.

36. Norman H. Snaith, *The Distinctive Ideas of the Old Testament,* p. 146.

37. *Ibid.,* p. 149.

38. Eichrodt, *Ezekiel,* p. 499.

39. Alexander Maclaren, *Expositions of Holy Scripture: Ezekiel, Daniel, and the Minor Prophets,* p. 21.

40. Feinberg, *Ezekiel,* p. 209.

41. *Ibid.,* p. 66.

42. Maclaren, *Ezekiel,* p. 22.

43. A. B. Davidson, *The Book of the Prophet Ezekiel,* p. 287.

44. Snaith, *Distinctive Ideas,* p. 154.

45. Ellison, *Ezekiel,* p. 128.

46. Dom Wulstan Mork, O.S.B. *The Biblical Meaning of Man,* pp. 79-80.

47. Feinberg, *Ezekiel,* p. 66.

48. E. H. Plumptre, "Ezekiel," of *The Pulpit Commentary,* I, 205.

49. Davidson, *Ezekiel,* p. 287.

50. John Skinner, "The Book of Ezekiel," of *The Expositor's Bible,* p. 337.

51. D. M. G. Stalker, "Ezekiel," of *Torch Bible Commentaries,* p. 115.

Chapter 4—THE NEW DISPOSITION, THE WORK OF THE LAW IN GENTILE HEARTS, AND REGENERATION

1. R. C. H. Lenski, *The Interpretation of St. Paul's Epistle to the Romans,* p. 165.

2. John Murray, "The Epistle to the Romans," Vol. I, in *The New International Commentary on the New Testament,* p. 75.

3. James M. Stifler, *The Epistle to the Romans,* p. 37.
4. L. Berkhof, *Systematic Theology,* p. 468.
5. *Ibid.,* p. 469.
6. Taken from *A Systematic Theology of the Christian Religion,* Vol. II, 168, by James Oliver Buswell. Copyright 1962 by Zondervan Publishing House. Used by permission.
7. Arthur W. Pink, *The Sovereignty of God,* p. 78.
8. Robert D. Knudsen, "The Nature of Regeneration," *Christian Faith and Modern Theology,* p. 316.
9. Berkhof, *Systematic Theology,* p. 473.
10. Pink, *Sovereignty,* p. 79.
11. Knudsen, "The Nature of Regeneration," p. 319.
12. William Hendriksen, "Exposition of the Pastoral Epistles," of *New Testament Commentary,* p. 391.
13. Henry Alford, *The Greek Testament,* III, 425.

Chapter 5—THE NEW DISPOSITION AND THE CHRISTIAN

1. John T. Demarest, *A Commentary on the Second Epistle of the Apostle Peter,* p. 89.
2. C. Leslie Mitton, "Romans—vii. Reconsidered—I, II, III" (here-inafter referred to as "Romans"), 78.
3. Anders Nygren, *Commentary on Romans,* p. 287.
4. Mitton, "Romans," p. 133.
5. For a thorough refutation of the other views see: Renald E. Showers, "The New Nature" (unpublished Th. D. dissertation, Grace Theological Seminary, 1975), pp. 90-101, 106.
6. F. F. Bruce, "The Epistle of Paul to the Romans," the *Tyndale New Testament Commentaries,* p. 150.
7. Nygren, *Commentary on Romans,* p. 286.
8. John Forbes, *Analytical Commentary on the Epistle to the Romans,* p. 287.
9. William R. Newell, *Romans Verse by Verse,* p. 277.
10. William G. T. Shedd, *A Critical and Doctrinal Commentary on the Epistle of St. Paul to the Romans,* p. 189.
11. For further arguments for the regenerate view see: Showers, "The New Nature," (unpublished dissertation, Grace Theological Seminary, 1975), pp. 101-105.

12. Marvin R. Vincent, *Word Studies in the New Testament,* III, 82.
13. *Ibid.*
14. John Murray, "The Epistle to the Romans," Vol. I, in the *New International Commentary on the New Testament,* p. 266.
15. Johannes Behm, "eso," *Theological Dictionary of the New Testament,* Vol. II, p. 699.

Chapter 6—THE BACKGROUND OF THE STRUGGLE OF THE CHRISTIAN

1. Kenneth Wuest, *Romans in the Greek New Testament,* p. 91.
2. Floyd Hamilton, *The Epistle to the Romans,* p. 98.
3. John Murray, "The Epistle to the Romans," Vol. I, in the *New International Commentary on the New Testament,* p. 233.
4. *Ibid.*
5. Werner Foerster, "kurios," *Theological Dictionary of the New Testament,* Vol. III, pp. 1040-1046.
6. Karl Heinrich Rengstorf, "doulos," *Theological Dictionary of the New Testament,* Vol. II, p. 261.
7. *Ibid.,* p. 270.
8. Charles R. Erdman, *The Epistle to the Romans,* p. 71.
9. Wuest, *Romans in the Greek New Testament,* p. 101.
10. Fred. Aug. Gottreu Tholuck, *Exposition of St. Paul's Epistle to the Romans,* p. 182.
11. G. G. Findlay, "St. Paul's First Epistle to the Corinthians," in Vol. II of the *Expositor's Greek Testament,* p. 931.
12. Wuest, *Romans in the Greek New Testament,* p. 98.
13. Charles Hodge, *An Exposition of the First Epistle to the Corinthians,* p. 339.
14. H. E. Dana and Julius R. Mantey, *A Manual Grammar of the Greek New Testament,* p. 84.
15. Marcus Rainsford, *Lectures on Romans,* Vol. VI, p. 46.
16. Friedrich Adolph Philippi, *Commentary on St. Paul's Epistle to the Romans,* Vol. I, p. 299.
17. Karl Barth, *A Shorter Commentary on Romans,* p. 69.
18. For refutations of the first three views see: Renald E. Showers, "The New Nature" (unpublished Th.D. dissertation, Grace Theological Seminary, 1975), pp. 136-38.

19. E. H. Gifford, *The Epistle of St. Paul to the Romans,* p. 128.
20. F. Godet, *Commentary on St. Paul's Epistle to the Romans,* Vol. I, p. 416.
21. Reprinted from *An Idiom-Book of New Testament Greek,* second edition, by C.F.D. Moule by permission of Cambridge University Press. Published by the syndics of The Cambridge University Press, 1960.
22. J. Oliver Buswell, *Ten Reasons Why a Christian Does Not Live a Wicked Life,* p. 20.
23. Richard Chenevix Trench, *Synonyms of the New Testament,* p. 30.
24. John Forbes, *Analytical Commentary on the Epistle to the Romans,* pp. 265-68.
25. Rainsford, *Lectures on Romans,* VI, 50.
26. *Ibid.*
27. William R. Newell, *Romans Verse by Verse,* p. 215.
28. Gifford, *The Epistle of St. Paul to the Romans,* p. 128.
29. William Sanday and Arthur C. Headlam, "A Critical and Exegetical Commentary on the Epistle to the Romans," in *International Critical Commentary,* p. 159.
30. Joseph Henry Thayer, *A Greek-English Lexicon of the New Testament,* p. 642.
31. *Ibid.*
32. David Brown, "The Epistle to the Romans," in the *Handbooks for Bible Classes,* p. 68.
33. For evidences for this conclusion see: Renald E. Showers, "The New Nature" (unpublished Th.D. dissertation, Grace Theological Seminary, 1975), pp. 160-62.
34. Charles Hodge, *Commentary on the Epistle to the Romans,* p. 217.
35. Trench, *Synonyms of the New Testament,* p. 220.
36. *Ibid.,* p. 253.
37. F. F. Bruce, "The Epistle of Paul to the Romans," in *Tyndale New Testament Commentaries,* p. 147.

Chapter 7—THE NEW DISPOSITION AND THE STRUGGLE OF THE CHRISTIAN

1. Anders Nygren, *Commentary on Romans,* pp. 293-302.
2. For a refutation of this view see: Renald E. Showers, "The New

Nature" (unpublished Th.D. dissertation, Grace Theological Seminary, 1975), pp. 179-182.

3. David N. Steele and Curtis C. Thomas, *Romans, an Interpretive Outline,* p. 56.

4. H. C. G. Moule, *The Epistle of Paul the Apostle to the Romans,* p. 132.

5. F. F. Bruce, "The Epistle of Paul to the Romans," in *Tyndale New Testament Commentaries,* p. 156.

6. H. E. Dana and Julius R. Mantey, *A Manual Grammar of the Greek New Testament,* p. 129.

7. Marvin R. Vincent, *Word Studies in the New Testament,* III, 80.

8. John A. T. Robinson, *The Body,* p. 19.

9. *Ibid.,* p. 20.

10. Vincent, *Word Studies,* III, 82.

11. William F. Arndt and F. Wilbur Gingrich, *A Greek-English Lexicon of the New Testament,* p. 797.

12. Vincent, *Word Studies,* III, 82.

13. John Murray, "The Epistle to the Romans," Vol. I, in *New International Commentary on the New Testament,* p. 266.

14. Gottlob Schrenk, "thelo," *Theological Dictionary of the New Testament,* Vol. III, p. 50.

15. *Ibid.,* p. 52.

16. Taken from *Plain Talk About Christian Words,* by Manford G. Gutzke. Copyright 1964 by Royal Publishers, Inc., copyright assigned to Zondervan Publishing House in 1965. Used by permission.

17. Charles Hodge, *Commentary on the Epistle to the Romans,* p. 230.

18. Robert Haldane, *Exposition of the Epistle to the Romans,* p. 304.

19. *Ibid.,* p. 305.

20. *Ibid.,* p. 294.

21. Murray, *The Epistle to the Romans,* I, 263.

22. William Kelly, *Notes on the Epistle of Paul, the Apostle, to the Romans,* p. 108.

23. Vincent, *Word Studies,* III, 84.

24. F. Godet, *Commentary on St. Paul's Epistle to the Romans,* 48.

25. Hodge, *Commentary on the Epistle to the Romans,* p. 238.

Chapter 8—THE NEW DISPOSITION AND THE HOLY SPIRIT

1. Norman H. Snaith, *The Distinctive Ideas of the Old Testament,* pp. 154-55.
2. *Ibid.,* p. 158.
3. *Ibid.,* p. 182-83.
4. *Ibid.,* p. 186.
5. Emil Brunner, *The Letter to the Romans,* p. 67.
6. F. F. Bruce, "The Epistle of Paul to the Romans," in *Tyndale New Testament Commentaries,* p. 159.
7. *Ibid.,* p. 160.
8. *Ibid.*
9. William G. T. Shedd, *A Critical and Doctrinal Commentary on the Epistle of St. Paul to the Romans,* p. 227.
10. John Murray, "The Epistle to the Romans," Vol. I, in *New International Commentary on the New Testament,* p. 278.
11. Friedrich Büchsel, "katakrino," *Theological Dictionary of the New Testament,* Vol. III, p. 951.
12. Murray, *The Epistle to the Romans,* I, 278.
13. F. Godet, *Commentary on St. Paul's Epistle to the Romans,* Vol. II, p. 66.
14. Homer A. Kent, Jr., *Ephesians: The Glory of the Church,* p. 58.
15. *Ibid.,* p. 59.
16. *Ibid.,* p. 60.
17. F. F. Bruce, *The Epistle to the Ephesians, p. 69.*

Chapter 9—THE NEW DISPOSITION, THE NEW MAN, AND THE IMAGE OF GOD AND CHRIST

1. Richard H. Bube, *A Textbook of Christian Doctrine,* p. 60.
2. Taken from *Plain Talk About Christian Words,* by Manford G. Gutzke, Copyright 1964 by Royal Publishers, Inc., copyright assigned to Zondervan Publishing House in 1965. Used by permission.
3. Robert Haldane, *Exposition of the Epistle to the Romans,* pp. 293-94.
4. Erich Sauer, *The King of the Earth,* p. 145.

Chapter 10—THE NEW DISPOSITION AND 1 JOHN 3:19

1. Albert Barnes, *Barnes' Notes on the New Testament,* p. 1482.
2. John H. A. Ebrard, *Biblical Commentary on the Epistles of St. John,* p. 227.
3. James M. Ghysels, *The Highest Fellowship,* p. 150.
4. Robert Law, *The Tests of Life,* p. 228.
5. Friedrich Lucke, *A Commentary on the Epistles of St. John,* p. 199.
6. George G. Findlay, *Fellowship in the Life Eternal,* p. 114.
7. W. E. Vine, *An Expository Dictionary of New Testament Words,* p. 339.
8. W. Robert Cook, "Hamartiological Problems in First John," *Bibliotheca Sacra,* p. 256.
9. Ebrard, *Biblical Commentary on the Epistles of St. John,* p. 234.
10. Lucke, *A Commentary on the Epistles of St. John,* p. 197.
11. *Ibid.,* p. 198.
12. Brooke Foss Westcott, *The Epistles of St. John,* p. 107.
13. A. R. Cocke, *Studies in the Epistles of John,* p. 78.
14. R. E. O. White, *Open Letter to Evangelicals,* p. 85.
15. Westcott, *The Epistles of St. John,* p. 107.
16. Guy H. King, *The Fellowship,* p. 74.
17. Law, *The Tests of Life,* p. 198.

Chapter 11—THE NEW DISPOSITION AND THE OLD TESTAMENT SAINT

1. John J. Davis, "Regeneration in the Old Testament" (unpublished Th.M. thesis, Grace Theological Seminary, 1964), p. 81.
2. *Ibid.,* p. 123.
3. F. C. Jennings, *Studies in Isaiah,* p. 592.

Chapter 12—THE NEW DISPOSITION AND THE OLD COVENANT LAW

1. J. Gresham Machen, *The Christian View of Man,* p. 185.
2. Gerhard Delling, "katargeo," *Theological Dictionary of the New Testament,* Vol. I, p. 454.

3. Robert Falconer, *The Pastoral Epistles,* p. 123.
4. Homer A. Kent, Jr., *The Pastoral Epistles,* p. 86.
5. William F. Arndt and F. Wilbur Gingrich, *A Greek-English Lexicon of the New Testament,* p. 71.
6. *Ibid.,* p. 266.
7. W. Gutbrod, "ennomos," *Theological Dictionary of the New Testament,* Vol. IV, p. 1087.

SELECT BIBLIOGRAPHY

Books

Alford, Henry. *The Greek Testament.* Chicago: Moody Press, 1958.

Anderson, Bernhard W. "The New Covenant and the Old." *The Old Testament and Christian Faith.* Edited by Bernhard W. Anderson. New York: Herder And Herder, 1969.

Arndt, William F., and Gingrich, F. Wilbur. *A Greek-English Lexicon of the New Testament and Other Early Christian Literature.* Chicago: The University of Chicago Press, 1957.

Barnes, Albert. *Barnes' Notes on the New Testament.* Grand Rapids: Kregel Publications, 1962.

Barnhouse, Donald Grey. *God's Freedom.* Grand Rapids: Wm. B. Eerdmans Publishing Company, 1961.

Barth, Karl. *A Shorter Commentary on Romans.* Richmond: John Knox Press, 1959.

———. *Church Dogmatics.* Edited by G. W. Bromiley and T. F. Torrance. Translated by Harold Knight, *et al.* 8 vols. Edinburgh: T. & T. Clark, 1960.

Beet, Joseph Agar. *A Commentary on St. Paul's Epistle to the Romans.* New York: Thomas Whittaker, 1901.

Behm, Johannes. "εσω." *Theological Dictionary of the New Testament.* Vols. I-IV edited by Gerhard Kittel; Vols. V-IX edited by Gerhard Friedrich. Translated and edited by Geoffrey W. Bromiley. Grand Rapids: Wm. B. Eerdmans Publishing Company, 1964-74.

_____. "καρδία ." *Theological Dictionary of the New Testament.* Vols. I-IV edited by Gerhard Kittel; Vols. V-IX edited by Gerhard Friedrich. Translated and edited by Geoffrey W. Bromiley. Grand Rapids: Wm. B. Eerdmans Publishing Company, 1964-74.

Bennett, W. H. "The Book of Jeremiah." *The Expositor's Bible.* Edited by W. Robertson Nicoll. 10 vols. New York: Funk & Wagnalls Company, 1900.

Berkhof, L. *Systematic Theology.* 4th rev. and enlarged ed. Grand Rapids: Wm. B. Eerdmans Publishing Company, 1962.

Bridges, Charles. *An Exposition of Proverbs.* London: The Banner of Truth Trust, 1968.

Brown, David. "The Epistle to the Romans." *Handbooks for Bible Classes.* Edited by Marcus Dods and Alexander Whyte. 44 vols. Edinburgh: T. & T. Clark, n.d.

Bruce, F. F. *The Epistle to the Ephesians.* London: Pickering & Inglis Ltd., 1961.

_____."The Epistle of Paul to the Romans." *The Tyndale New Testament Commentaries.* Edited by R. V. G. Tasker. 19 vols. Grand Rapids: Wm. B. Eerdmans Publishing Company, 1957—.

_____."The Epistle to the Hebrews." *The New International Commentary on the New Testament.* Edited by F. F. Bruce. 19 vols. Grand Rapids: Wm. B. Eerdmans Publishing Company, 1949—.

Brunner, Emil. *Man in Revolt.* London: Lutterworth Press, 1939.

_____. *The Letter to the Romans.* London: Lutterworth Press, 1959.

Bube, Richard H. *A Textbook of Christian Doctrine.* Chicago: Moody Press, 1955.

Büchsel, Friedrich. "κατακρίνω ." *Theological Dictionary of the New Testament.* Vols. I-IV edited by Gerhard Kittel;

Vols. V-IX edited by Gerhard Friedrich. Translated and edited by Geoffrey W. Bromiley. Grand Rapids: Wm. B. Eerdmans Publishing Company, 1964-74.

Buswell, James Oliver, Jr. *A Systematic Theology of the Christian Religion.* Grand Rapids: Zondervan Publishing House, 1962.

_____. *Ten Reasons Why a Christian Does Not Live a Wicked Life.* Chicago: Moody Press, 1959.

Calvin, John. *Commentaries on the Book of the Prophet Ezekiel.* Translated and edited by Thomas Myers. Grand Rapids: Wm. B. Eerdmans Publishing Company, 1948.

_____.*Commentaries on the Book of the Prophet Jeremiah and the Lamentations.* Translated and edited by John Owen. Grand Rapids: Wm. B. Eerdmans Publishing Company, 1950.

Cauthen, Kenneth. *The Impact of American Religious Liberalism.* New York: Harper & Row, 1962.

Cheyne, T. K., and Adeney, W. F. "Jeremiah." *The Pulpit Commentary.* Edited by H. D. M. Spence and Joseph S. Exell. 51 vols. New York: Funk & Wagnalls Company, 1913.

Cocke, A. R. *Studies in the Epistles of John.* Richmond, Va.: The Presbyterian Committee of Publication, 1895.

Cotton, John. *An Exposition of First John.* Evansville, Ind.: Sovereign Grace Publishers, n.d.

Cowles, Henry. *Jeremiah, and His Lamentations.* New York: D. Appleton and Company, 1853.

Cunliffe-Jones, H. "The Book of Jeremiah." *Torch Bible Commentaries.* Edited by John Marsh and Alan Richardson. 30 vols. London: SCM Press Ltd., 1948—.

Dana, H. E., and Mantey, Julius R. *A Manual Grammar of the Greek New Testament.* New York: The Macmillan Company, 1927; renewed 1955 by Tommie P. Dana and Julius R. Mantey.

Davidson, A. B. *The Book of the Prophet Ezekiel.* Cambridge: University Press, 1924.

Delling, Gerhard. "καταργέω ." *Theological Dictionary of the New Testament.* Vols. I-IV edited by Gerhard Kittel; Vols. V-IX edited by Gerhard Friedrich. Translated and edited by Geoffrey W. Bromiley. Grand Rapids: Wm. B. Eerdmans Publishing Company, 1964-74.

Demarest, John T. *A Commentary on the Second Epistle of the Apostle Peter.* New York: Sheldon & Co., 1862.

Ebrard, John H. A. *Biblical Commentary on the Epistles of St. John.* Translated by W. B. Pope. Edinburgh: T. & T. Clark, 1860.

Eichrodt, Walther. *Ezekiel.* Philadelphia: The Westminster Press, 1970.

_____. *Theology of the Old Testament.* Philadelphia: The Westminster Press. 1967.

Ellison, H. L. *Ezekiel: The Man and His Message.* Grand Rapids: Wm. B. Eerdmans Publishing Company, 1956.

Erdman, Charles R. *The Epistle to the Romans.* Grand Rapids: Baker Book House, 1983.

Falconer, Robert. *The Pastoral Epistles.* Oxford: The Clarendon Press, 1937.

Feinberg, Charles Lee. *The Prophecy of Ezekiel.* Chicago: Moody Press, 1970.

Ferme, Charles. *A Logical Analysis of the Epistle of Paul to the Romans.* Translated by Wm. Skae. Edited by Wm. Lindsay Alexander. Edinburgh: The Wodrow Society, 1850.

Findlay, G. G. *Fellowship in the Life Eternal.* Grand Rapids: Wm. B. Eerdmans Publishing Company, 1955.

_____. "St. Paul's First Epistle to the Corinthians." *The Expositor's Greek Testament.* Edited by W. Robertson Nicoll. 5 vols. Grand Rapids: Wm. B. Eerdmans Publishing Company, n.d.

Foerster, Werner. "κύριο s." *Theological Dictionary of the New*

Testament. Vols. I-IV edited by Gerhard Kittel; Vols. V-IX edited by Gerhard Friedrich. Translated and edited by Geoffrey W. Bromiley. Grand Rapids: Wm. B. Eerdmans Publishing Company, 1964-74.

Forbes, John. *Analytical Commentary on the Epistle to the Romans.* Edinburgh: T. & T. Clark, 1868.

Fretheim, Terence E. *Creation, Fall, and Flood.* Minneapolis: Augsburg Publishing House, 1969.

Gaebelein, A. C. *The Annotated Bible;* one volume edition entitled *Gaebelein's Concise Commentary on the Whole Bible.* Neptune, New Jersey: Loizeaux Brothers, revised edition, 1985.

Ghysels, James M. *The Highest Fellowship.* Grand Rapids: Zondervan Publishing House, 1936.

Gifford, E. H. *The Epistle of St. Paul to the Romans.* London: John Murray, 1886.

Gill, John. *An Exposition of the Old Testament.* Vol. V: *The Book of the Prophet Isaiah, The Book of the Prophet Jeremiah.* Philadelphia: William W. Woodward, 1818.

Godet, F. *Commentary on St. Paul's Epistle to the Romans.* Translated by A. Cusin. Edinburgh: T. & T. Clark, 1895.

Gray, James Comper. *The Biblical Museum.* New York: Anson D. F. Randolph & Company, n.d.

Grundmann, Walter. "ἁμαρτάνω ." *Theological Dictionary of the New Testament.* Vols. I-IV edited by Gerhard Kittel; Vols. V-IX edited by Gerhard Friedrich. Translated and edited by Geoffrey W. Bromiley. Grand Rapids: Wm. B. Eerdmans Publishing Company, 1964-74.

Gutbrod, W. "νόμο s, ἄνομο s, ἔννομο s, νομοθετέω ." *Theological Dictionary of the New Testament.* Vols. I-IV edited by Gerhard Kittel; Vols. V-IX edited by Gerhard Friedrich. Translated and edited by Geoffrey W. Bromiley. Grand Rapids: Wm. B. Eerdmans Publishing Company, 1964-74.

Gutzke, Manford George. *Plain Talk about Christian Words.* Grand Rapids: Zondervan Publishing House, 1965.

Habel, Norman C. "Jeremiah, Lamentations." *Concordia Commentary.* Edited by Walter J. Bartling and Albert E. Glock. 4 vols. Saint Louis: Concordia Publishing House, 1968—.

Haldane, Robert. *Exposition of the Epistle to the Romans.* London: The Banner of Truth Trust, 1960.

Hamilton, Floyd E. *The Epistle to the Romans.* Grand Rapids: Baker Book House, 1958.

Haupt, Erich. *The First Epistle of St. John.* Translated by W. B. Pope. Edinburgh: T. & T. Clark, 1879.

Henderson, E. *The Book of the Prophet Jeremiah and That of the Lamentations.* Andover: Warren F. Draper, 1868.

Hendriksen, William. "Exposition of the Pastoral Epistles." *New Testament Commentary.* 7 vols. Grand Rapids: Baker Book House, 1953—.

Hengstenberg, E. W. *Christology of the Old Testament.* Grand Rapids: Kregel Publications, 1956.

Henry, Carl F. H. "Man." *Baker's Dictionary of Theology.* Edited by Everett F. Harrison. Grand Rapids: Baker Book House, 1960.

Henry, Matthew. *Matthew Henry's Commentary on the Whole Bible.* Vol. IV: "Jeremiah To Malachi." New York: Fleming H. Revell Company, n.d.

Hodge, Charles. *Commentary on the Epistle to the Romans.* New ed. Grand Rapids: Wm. B. Eerdmans Publishing Company, 1955.

_____. *An Exposition of the First Epistle to the Corinthians.* London: The Banner of Truth Trust, 1959.

Jamieson, Robert; Fausset, A. R.; and Brown, David. *A Commentary, Critical, Experimental, And Practical, on the Old and New Testaments.* Philadelphia: J. B. Lippincott & Co., n.d.

Jennings, F. C. *Studies in Isaiah.* Neptune, New Jersey: Loizeaux Brothers, Inc., 1950.

Keil, Carl Friedrich. *Biblical Commentary on the Prophecies of Ezekiel.* Translated by James Martin. *Biblical Commentary on the Old Testament.* By C. F. Keil and Franz Delitzsch. 25 vols. Grand Rapids: Wm. B. Eerdmans Publishing Company, 1949-50.

_____. "The Prophecies of Jeremiah." Translated by David Patrick. *Biblical Commentary on the Old Testament.* By C. F. Keil and Franz Delitzsch. 25 vols. Grand Rapids: Wm. B. Eerdmans Publishing Company, 1949-50.

Kelly, William. *Notes on the Epistle of Paul, the Apostle, to the Romans.* n.p., 1873.

Kent, Homer A., Jr. *Ephesians: The Glory of the Church.* Chicago: Moody Press, 1971.

_____. *The Pastoral Epistles.* Chicago: Moody Press, 1958.

King, Guy H. *The Fellowship.* London: Marshall, Morgan & Scott Ltd., 1956.

Klooster, Fred H. "The Nature of Man," in *Christian Faith and Modern Theology.* Edited by Carl F. H. Henry. Grand Rapids: Baker Book House, 1971.

Knudsen, Robert D. "The Nature of Regeneration," in *Christian Faith and Modern Theology.* Grand Rapids: Baker Book House, 1971.

Knudson, Albert Cornelius. *The Doctrine of Redemption.* Nashville: Abingdon Press, 1933.

Kuist, Howard Tillman. "The Book of Jeremiah, The Lamentations of Jeremiah." Vol. XII of *The Layman's Bible Commentary.* Edited by Balmer H. Kelly. 25 vols. Richmond, Va.: John Knox Press, 1959—.

Laetsch, Theo. *Jeremiah.* Saint Louis: Concordia Publishing House, 1952.

Law, Robert. *The Tests of Life.* Grand Rapids: Baker Book House, 1968.

Lenski, R. C. H. *The Interpretation of St. Paul's Epistle to the Romans.* Minneapolis: Augsburg Publishing House, 1961.

Liddell, George Henry, and Scott, Robert. *A Greek-English Lexicon.* New Ed. Oxford: The University Press, 9th ed., 1940.

Liddon, H. P. *Explanatory Analysis of St. Paul's Epistle to the Romans.* 3rd ed. London: Longmans, Green, and Co., 1897.

Lightfoot, J. B. *The Epistle of St. Paul to the Galatians.* Grand Rapids: Zondervan Publishing House, 1957.

Lucke, Friedrich. *A Commentary on the Epistles of St. John.* Translated by Thorlief Gudmundson Repp. Edinburgh: Thomas Clark, 1837.

Machen, J. Gresham. *The Christian View of Man.* Edinburgh: The Banner of Truth Trust, 1965.

_____. *New Testament Greek for Beginners.* New York: The Macmillan Company, 1953.

Maclaren, Alexander. *Expositions of Holy Scripture. Ezekiel, Daniel, and the Minor Prophets.* New York: Hodder & Stoughton, n.d.

Matthews, Shailer. *The Gospel and Modern Man.* New York: The Macmillan Company, 1910.

Mork, Dom Wulstan. *The Biblical Meaning of Man.* New York: The Macmillan Publishing Company, 1967.

Moule, C. F. D. Reprinted from *An Idiom-Book of New Testament Greek,* 2nd ed. Cambridge: Cambridge University Press, 1960.

Moule, H. C. G. "The Epistle of Paul the Apostle to the Romans." *The Cambridge Bible for Schools And Colleges.* 49 vols. Cambridge: The University Press, 1885—.

Moulton, James Hope, and Milligan, George. *The Vocabulary of the Greek Testament.* Grand Rapids: Wm. B. Eerdmans Publishing Company, 1949.

Moulton, James Hope. *Prolegomena. A Grammar of New Testament Greek.* 2 vols. Edinburgh: T. & T. Clark, 1957.

Murray, John. *Principles of Conduct.* Grand Rapids: Wm. B. Eerdmans Publishing Company, 1957.

————. "The Epistle to the Romans." *The New International Commentary on the New Testament.* Edited by Ned B. Stonehouse. 19 vols. Grand Rapids: Wm. B. Eerdmans Publishing Company, 1949—.

Naegelsbach, C. W. Eduard. "The Book of the Prophet Jeremiah." Vol. XII of *A Commentary on the Holy Scriptures.* Translated and edited by Philip Schaff. 24 vols. New York: Charles Scribner's Sons, 1915.

Newell, William R. *Romans, Verse by Verse.* Chicago: Moody Press, 1938.

Niebuhr, Reinhold. *The Nature and Destiny of Man.* New York: Charles Scribner's Sons, 1941.

————. "Sin." *A Handbook of Christian Theology.* Edited by Marvin Halverson and Arthur A. Cohen. New York: Meridian Books, Inc., 1958.

Nygren, Anders. *Commentary on Romans.* Translated by Carl C. Rasmussen. Philadelphia: Muhlenberg Press, 1949.

Orelli, C. Von. *The Prophecies of Jeremiah.* Edinburgh: T. & T. Clark, 1889.

Philippi, Friedrich Adolph. *Commentary on St. Paul's Epistle to the Romans.* Translated by J. S. Banks. Edinburgh: T. & T. Clark, 1878.

Pink, Arthur W. *The Sovereignty of God.* London: The Banner of Truth Trust, 1961.

Plumptre, E. H. *Ezekiel. The Pulpit Commentary.* Edited by H. D. M. Spence and Joseph S. Exell. 51 vols. New York: Funk & Wagnalls Company, 1913.

Rainsford, Marcus. *Lectures on Romans.* London: John Hoby, n.d.

Rainy, Robert. "The Epistle to the Philippians." *The Exposi-*

tor's Bible. Edited by W. Robertson Nicoll. 10 vols. New York: Funk & Wagnalls Company, 1900.

Rauschenbusch, Walter. *Christianizing the Social Order*. New York: The Macmillan Company, 1912.

_____. *A Theology for the Social Gospel*. New York: The Macmillan Company, 1917.

Rengstorf, Karl Heinrich. "δουλος." *Theological Dictionary of the New Testament*. Vols. I-IV edited by Gerhard Kittel; Vols. V-IX edited by Gerhard Friedrich. Translated and edited by Geoffrey W. Bromiley. Grand Rapids: Wm. B. Eerdmans Publishing Company, 1964-74.

Robinson, John A. T. *The Body*. London: SCM Press Ltd., 1961.

Sanday, W., and Headlam, A. C. "A Critical and Exegetical Commentary on the Epistle to the Romans." *The International Critical Commentary*. Edited by Charles Augustus Briggs, Samuel Rolles Driver, and Alfred Plummer. 48 vols. New York: Charles Scribner's Sons, 1910—.

Sartre, Jean-Paul. *The Philosophy of Existentialism*. New York: Philosophical Library, 1965.

Sauer, Erich. *The King of the Earth*. Grand Rapids: Wm. B. Eerdmans Publishing Company, 1962.

Schrenk, Gottlob, "θἑλω ." *Theological Dictionary of the New Testament*. Vols. I-IV edited by Gerhard Kittel; Vols. V-IX edited by Gerhard Friedrich. Translated and edited by Geoffrey W. Bromiley. Grand Rapids: Wm. B. Eerdmans Publishing Company, 1964-74.

Shedd, William G. T. *Dogmatic Theology*. Grand Rapids: Zondervan Publishing House, n.d.

_____. *A Critical and Doctrinal Commentary on the Epistle of St. Paul to the Romans*. Grand Rapids: Zondervan Publishing House, 1967.

Skinner, John. "The Book of Ezekiel" *The Expositor's Bible*. Edited by W. Robertson Nicoll. 10 vols. New York: Funk & Wagnalls Company, 1900.

Snaith, Norman H. *The Distinctive Ideas of the Old Testament.* New York: Schocken Books, 1964; Epworth Press, London, 1944 and 1983.

Stählin, Gustav. "αμαρτάνω ." *Theological Dictionary of the New Testament.* Vols. I-IV edited by Gerhard Kittel; Vols. V-IX edited by Gerhard Friedrich. Translated and edited by Geoffrey W. Bromiley. Grand Rapids: Wm. B. Eerdmans Publishing Company, 1964-74.

Stalker, D. M. G. "Ezekiel." *Torch Bible Commentaries.* Edited by John Marsh and Alan Richardson. 30 vols. London: SCM Press Ltd., 1948—.

Steele, David N., and Thomas, Curtis C. *Romans, An Interpretive Outline.* Philadelphia: The Presbyterian and Reformed Publishing Company, 1963.

Stifler, James M. *The Epistle to the Romans.* New York: Fleming H. Revell Company, 1897.

Streane, A. W. "The Book of the Prophet Jeremiah." *The Cambridge Bible For Schools and Colleges.* 49 vols. Cambridge: The University Press, 1885—.

Strong, Augustus Hopkins. *Systematic Theology.* Westwood, N.J.: Fleming H. Revell Company, 1954.

Taylor, John B. "Ezekiel." *The Tyndale Old Testament Commentaries.* Edited by D. J. Wiseman. 4 vols. Downers Grove, Ill.: Inter-Varsity Press, 1964—.

Thayer, Joseph Henry. *A Greek-English Lexicon of the New Testament.* Grand Rapids: Zondervan Publishing House, 1977.

Tholuck, Fred. Aug. Gottreu. *Exposition of St. Paul's Epistle to the Romans.* Translated by Robert Menzies. Philadelphia: Sorin and Ball, 1844.

Trapp, John. *A Commentary on the Old and New Testaments.* Vol. III: "Proverbs of Solomon-Daniel." London: Richard D. Dickinson, 1868.

Trench, Richard Chenevix. *Synonyms of the New Testament.* London: Macmillan and Co., 1865.

Van Til, Cornelius. *The Defense of the Faith.* Philadelphia: The Presbyterian and Reformed Publishing Company, 1955.

Vincent, Marvin R. *Word Studies in the New Testament.* Vol. III: "The Epistles of Paul." Grand Rapids: Wm. B. Eerdmans Publishing Company, 1957.

Vine, W. E. *An Expository Dictionary of New Testament Words.* London: Oliphants, Ltd., 1961.

Westcott, Brooke Foss. *The Epistles of St. John.* Grand Rapids: Wm. B. Eerdmans Publishing Company, 1957.

What, Then, Is Man? St. Louis: Concordia Publishing House, 1958.

White, R. E. O. *Open Letter to Evangelicals.* Grand Rapids: Wm. B. Eerdmans Publishing Company, 1964.

Wuest, Kenneth. *Romans in the Greek New Testament.* Grand Rapids: Wm. B. Eerdmans Publishing Company, 1956.

Young, Edward J. *Genesis 3.* London: The Banner of Truth Trust, 1966.

Encyclopedia Articles

Brennan, S. O'Flynn. "Nature." *New Catholic Encyclopedia.* 1967. Vol. X.

"Humanity." *A Catholic Dictionary.* 1961. 3rd ed.

Lewis, Charlton T., and Short, Charles. "natura." *A Latin Dictionary.* 1958.

"Nature." *The American College Dictionary.* 1948. Text ed.

"Nature." *The Oxford English Dictionary.* 1961. Vol. VII.

"Nature." *The Zondervan Pictorial Bible Dictionary.* 1963.

"Nature." *Webster's Third New International Dictionary.* 1981.

Oesterle, J. A. "Human Act." *New Catholic Encyclopedia.* 1967. Vol. VII.

Parenti, Pietro; Piolanti, Antonio; and Garofalo, Salvatore. "Person." *Dictionary of Dogmatic Theology.* 1951.

———. "Substance." *Dictionary of Dogmatic Theology.* 1951.

Rosenblatt, Samuel. "Inclination, Good And Evil." *Encyclopaedia Judaica.* 1972. Vol. VIII.

Journal Articles

Cook, W. Robert. "Hamartiological Problems in First John." *Bibliotheca Sacra,* CXXIII (July-September, 1966), 256.

Mitton, C. Leslie. "Romans—vii. Reconsidered—I, II, III." *The Expository Times,* 65 (October, 1953—September, 1954), 78.

Toussaint, Stanley D. "The Contrast Between the Spiritual Conflict in Romans 7 and Galatians 5." *Bibliotheca Sacra,* CXXIII (October-December, 1966), 310-14.

Towns, Elmer. "The Meaning of Heart in the New Testament," *Grace Journal,* XII (Winter, 1971), 36-45.

Unpublished Materials

Davis, John J. "Regeneration in the Old Testament." Unpublished Th.M. thesis, Grace Theological Seminary, 1964.

Firl, Robert L. "In My Flesh Dwelleth No Good Thing—Romans 7:18." Unpublished M.Div. critical monograph, Grace Theological Seminary, 1962.

Johnson, S. Lewis. "A Survey of Biblical Psychology in the Epistle to the Romans." Unpublished Th.D. dissertation, Dallas Theological Seminary, 1949.